SECRET
ABERDEEN

Lorna Corall Dey

AMBERLEY

First published 2016

Amberley Publishing
The Hill, Stroud
Gloucestershire, GL5 4EP

www.amberley-books.com

ISBN 978 1 4456 4914 6 (print)
ISBN 978 1 4456 4915 3 (ebook)

British Library Cataloguing in Publication Data.
A catalogue record for this book is available from the
British Library.

Typesetting by Amberley Publishing.
Printed in Great Britain.

Contents

Preface

Aberdeen, the city that can claim the oldest corporation in Scotland with royal charters dating back to William the Lion in the twelfth century, a council as ancient as 1398 and said to be one of the finest-built cities in the world, with Union Street among 'the most magnificent thoroughfares in the empire' is a city not given to boasting. This book aims to shed light on some lesser-known aspects of humble Aberdeen, sometimes forgotten, sometimes ignored.

1. As Heaven Gives Me So I Give Thee

Whether for grog or tea, bathing or laundry or a cure for ailments – water, as William Cadenhead, poet and vintner, noted in *The Book of Bon-Accord* of 1853, is a precious commodity.

We forget how relatively recent the luxury of clean water on tap is. Until the twentieth century households and trades were dependent on common burns, rivers, springs and wells for supplies, often intermittent, which had to be drawn and carried home by jug and pail. The loch that gave its name to Loch Street was of little use as it tended to dry up during summer and in any case became polluted with discharges from nearby industries, such as dyers and from the detritus running in from gutters.

Given the difficulty of obtaining good water it is little wonder that the preferred thirst quencher was often home-brewed ale but we cannot live by beer alone, although a few have tried. Wells and fountains were built over springs and burns to ease the collection of water, some simple spouts others more elaborate. Most have disappeared from our streets with a few retained as decorative features at roadsides and parks and one or two place names recall those times – Fountainhall, Marywell and Spa Streets.

A typical old street fountain.

So vital is water that wells were sometimes dedicated to saints in gratitude and to safeguard continued supplies from these holy wells. St Mary's Well at Affleck Street, dedicated to the Virgin Mary, no longer exists but something of St John's Well does.

In fact there were two St John's wells in Aberdeen. One at Old Aberdeen supplied St Machar's Cathedral for baptisms and washing church artefacts and another stood on land at Gilcomston, known as St John's Croft. The latter was the property of the Knights of St John, whose hospital here the well served along with more recent inhabitants of Skene Row, the Hardweird and Jack's Brae. When Rosemount Viaduct was being built the well was relocated to Albyn Place.

The Angel Well, named after the archangel Michael whose attribute of healing is little remembered, once provided water at Hanover Street and it may be that it was dug by William Ranaldson and his neighbours who were granted permission to excavate a well at the Thieves' or Justice Port in 1558:

> neyr the theyffs port to big ane draw well to serff thame of watter
> the same to be biggit with ane wall of stane and lyme of six futt
> leynth abou the erd to sauff all bairins and bestiall fra danger...

Still very visible, though dry, is a fragment of the Well o' Spa now at the corner of Spa and Skene Streets. Once it stood closer to the former Woolmanhill Infirmary and its healing waters might have encouraged the building of the hospital there as it was no ordinary well with its chalybeate or iron-rich waters, valued for their medicinal qualities.

Aberdeen's first mediciner, Gilbert Skene or Skeyne, physician to James VI, wrote:

Ane Brief Descriptioun of the Qualities, and Effectis of the

St John's Well, now on Albyn Place.

The old dam at Gilcomston.

Thieves' or Justice Port now Justice Street where remains of those executed on the Gallow hills were preserved and displayed as a deterrent.

Well of the Womanhill besyde Abirdene, Anno Do. 1580

The work is remarkable as a scholarly text written in the vernacular, in Doric not Latin as was customary, and the second such published in Scotland; the first was also Skene's work – his famous treatise of 1568 on the plague, the first essay on the Black Death written in English. Vernacular prose allowed non-Latin readers to access information about health matters.

To Skene the Well o' Spa was, 'ane ornament and ane publict utilitie to the Realme & Burgh' and he enhanced its reputation through reference to the fathers of medicine, Galen and Hippocrates. Although Skene compared it to the famous sulphurous hot springs at Aachen the well was named after the Belgian town of Spa, itself renowned for its mineral waters.

The eminent Dr William Barclay called the Well o' Spa 'the nymph of Aberdene, Callirhoe', after the daughter of the Greek god Oceanus and for Barclay, too, the Spa was a treasure of health. A northeasterner and professor at the University of Paris, Barclay is famous for his pamphlet of 1614 in praise of tobacco which drew a rebuke from James VI in his response *A Counterblaste to Tobacco*. To validate his claims for the Spa's beneficial qualities Barclay dropped an oak nutgall into a container of its water. Instead of turning black the water became as red as claret wine to the doctor's delight.

Barclay, like many, believed individual character was determined by an excess of one of four bodily fluids or humours: phlegm, yellow bile, black bile or blood. Northern types were regarded as phlegmatic due to the North's colder, wetter climate and with a tendency towards rheumatism, catarrh and digestive problems which might be counteracted by the

Remains of the Well o' Spa at Lower Skene Street.

ingestion of hot and drying substances of which iron-rich water was one.

The Spa of all local wells attracted greatest praise, not least from the celebrated painter George Jamesone, Scotland's Vandyke who lived nearby in Schoolhill and who had the well repaired and provided with a protective canopy, 'a vault of hewn stone over this spring' in 1635 in gratitude for the relief it gave him for calculus of the bladder (kidney stones).

A few short years later the spring was buried by the Denburn in spate and for thirty years was rendered useless until Baillie Alexander Skene had it reinstated in red sandstone.

The Spa, too, was the subject of many verses of varying quality. In 1903 Aberdeen's Chief Constable William Anderson wrote these words:

> But I hae had a notion lang
> The Infirmary fowk gaed me a bang,
> An' set my springs for envy wrang,
> Because they saw
> I cured the hale complainin' gang
> For nought ava.

So there – no need to visit the infirmary when taking the water was as effective. The remnant of the Well o' Spa is without its carvings of the apostles and the prosaic lines:

> The stomach, Reins, the Liver, Spleen, yea sure
> A thousand evils this wholesome Spring doth cure.

Portraitist and father of British art, George Jamesone's house on Schoolhill, once manse for St Nicholas Kirk (courtesy of Aberdeen City Libraries).

However efficacious the waters of Spa were they were powerless to prevent the encroachment of the Northern railway line which sealed its source and its fate.

Nearby but less salubrious was the Corbie Haugh Well serving Mutton Brae until its source, the Denburn, became a 'broad filthy current of ditch water' from bleaching greens and sundry industries along its banks. With the creation of Union Terrace Gardens or Trainie Park as it was known because of the railway running alongside, pollution, the well and the Denburn were removed, from sight at least.

Fidler's Well reminds us that individuals were also important in providing public water, including for animals. Coal broker Alex (Sandy) Fidler dedicated his well on Guild Street to Dr William Guild, once principal at King's College who, as the dedication on the well explains, died on Lammas day 1 August 1657 and the well was erected on the bicentenary of Dr Guild's death, in August 1857.

> Water springs for man and beast
> at your service I am here
> although six thousand years of age
> I am caller clean and clear.

 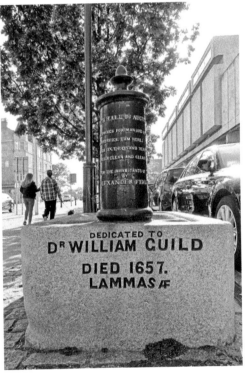

Above left: Corby Haugh Well.

Above right: Fidler's Well dedicated to Dr William Guild, founder and first patron of the Seven Incorporated Trades of Aberdeen.

The trough which was popular with carters carrying goods around the town, harbour and railway for refreshing their horses also had iron cups secured with chains that humans could also slake their thirst. The bonny Fidler's Well now stands dry on Holburn Street outside the Incorporated Trades Hall.

Farther afield at Sunnybank was the Firhill or Gibberie Wallie, pronounced with a hard 'g', its name derived from gingerbread sellers who used it as their pitch. In the 1930s the Wallie was moved during redevelopments to the Sunnybank allotments.

Not so far from the Gibberie Wallie was the Kittybrewster Well, erected by Jane Forbes Taylor to commemorate her father, Alex, a woollen draper in the town. A fine polished granite fountain it is now in Duthie Park and, like Fidler's, was built with animals as well as humans in mind: a horse trough on one side, a drinking spout for people and street level bowl for dogs.

With people moving into Aberdeen to find work the city's authorities were pressured into improving amenities: street lighting, cleaning and water supplies. They created a network of pipes linking springs with fountain or cistern houses and wells. Where once water pressure of 20 gallons per minute had sufficed increased demand on supplies led to improvements to over 100 gallons by the 1790s and the number of wells was increased from nine to twenty-seven.

The Castle Street Well or Mannie played an important role in the introduction of piped water to Aberdeen. This 1708 fountain has led an itinerant life; starting in the Castlegate he moved to the Green and is now back in the Castlegate, or nearly. Three hundred years

Gibberie Wallie.

Left: Taylor's Well with dog bowl.

Below: Taylor's Well with horse trough.

The Mannie or
Castle Street
fountain.

ago William Lindsay, overseer of water arranged the conveyance of spring water from Cardensheugh (Carden Place) to reservoirs at Fountainhall then to the Water-house at Broad Street and finally to the Mannie through lead pipes.

The Mannie's sophisticated engineering belied his humble appearance although original plans were for several gilded figures to adorn the fountain but money ran out. Water was disgorged at each corner of the sandstone wellhead from the mouths of carved Green Men and from a single lionhead-shaped spout. In 1852 the Mannie became a deluxe fountain when by the turn of a handle it could provide either spring or river water.

Improvements to the city's water system increased its quantity and purity. A new cistern was built towards the west end of Union Street, at Union Place, and in 1829 when the city's daily water consumption was around 0.4 million gallons it was granted parliamentary permission to pump River Dee water into various wells, fountains and cisterns across the town. River water was filtered through sand and pumped by steam engines at something like 1,000 gallons per minute with the potential of over one million gallons daily flowing into the cistern at Union Place. By 1862 the city was drawing five million gallons each day from the River Dee at Invercanny 22 miles away, via a brick aqueduct, to Aberdeen's cisterns. This vastly improved system cost the city £100,000, multiple-millions in today's money, yet did not cost local tax payers any additional rates.

Very gradually houses and tenements were fitted with their own water supplies and fountains and wells became redundant. Take time to admire those that remain and be grateful for the water on tap in your home.

Eighteenth-century Fountainhall cistern (courtesy of Aberdeen City Libraries).

The Fountainhall cistern as preserved in Duthie Park.

Broad Street in 1833 showing the waterhouse with clock, archway to Marischal College and close-by Byron's house at No. 64 (courtesy of Aberdeen City Libraries).

DID YOU KNOW?

When the waterhouse at Broad Street was built it obscured the dial-plate or clock on Marischal College so a new clock made by the Copper Company of Aberdeen was attached to the exterior of the building. This clock which would have been familiar to Aberdeen loon George Gordon, later Lord Byron, who lived almost next door to it, now graces the City Hospital tower.

Aberdeen's fire engine was once stored, appropriately, beneath the Broad Street Waterhouse.

2. Gentlemen Drank Deep

In Aberdeen drinking places were more likely to be known by the name of their licensee than a given-name for the premises and might be one reason painted signs over inns and taverns were a rare sight in the city and why Daniel Defoe struggled to find somewhere to drink during a visit, for there was no shortage of drinking houses. He did eventually find solace in the Change House.

The Scots' fondness for drink is well known. Joannes Scotus, the fifteenth-century philosopher, when asked by King Charles the Bold of France, the difference between a Scot and a sot replied, 'Only the breadth of the table.'

Mindful of such a reputation Aberdeen magistrates ordered the Marischal College bell be rung to signal a 10.00 p.m. liquor curfew in 1606. Nevertheless centuries later it was still a case of, 'gentlemen drank deep,' consuming wines and ales by the quart or indeed the magnum when it came to claret for those with the means. It was claimed a comprehensive list of liquor purveyors could be compiled from Marischal College's refectory accounts and from gown to town the burghers of Aberdeen were 'no dry-lipped generation'. To deter drunkenness the town council imposed in 1625 a fine of 40 pound Scots on anyone guilty of forcing wine or beer on a drinking companion against his wishes, a huge sum and clearly meant as a deterrent.

Painted sign over the Frigate Bar on the Netherkirkgate.

STANLEY HOTEL

TRY SILVER BELL WHISKY

He won't be Happy till he gets a drop.

Cartoon of the harbour's Stanley Hotel once run by the mother of Robert Williams, later Sir Robert Williams, friend of Cecil Rhodes and engineer involved in construction of the Katanga railway.

Aberdeen's taverns or howffs were mainly frequented by men although brewers, innkeepers and spirit dealers were frequently women as an 1854 list demonstrates: Mrs Burnett at the Royal Oak on Carmelite Street; Martha Gorard of the Burns tavern on the Guestrow; Mrs McKay at the Littlejohn Street tavern; Mrs Riach of the Workman's tavern, Shiprow; Agnes Snowie of Huxter Row's Rising Sun; Mrs (Ma) Cameron of the eighteenth-century coaching inn, originally the Sow Croft; and the estimable Mrs Ronald of the Lemon Tree.

There have been several Lemon Tree taverns in Aberdeen. The original was next to the watch-house on Huxter Row and advertised itself as the 'Oldest Established Commercial and best Dining House in Aberdeen'. In *Reporting Reminiscences* William Carnie recalled 'such creamy Finnan haddocks, such magnificent partan claws' and Mrs Ronald's retirement was marked by a lavish celebration she attended in her 'amplest black silk gown, snow-white set up cap, hand bag over her arm'. Following her departure Isaac Machray of the Prince of Wales Restaurant then added the Lemon Tree to his empire of inns and hostelries.

As today, taverns were distinguished by their entertainment along with the quality of food and drink. Aberdeen's drinking houses were reputedly hugely sociable affairs, very lively with music and storytelling, with Affleck's tucked into a close at Exchequer Row regarded as one of the best. Along with the disappearance of the Duffus hotel by the Guestrow went the traditional tappit hens – pewter lidded ale jugs and gill-stoups – the narrow drinking vessels that held a gill or quarter pint of spirits.

The original Lemon Tree on Huxter Row (demolished to make way for the Town House). Note a gas street lamp connected to a freestanding gas pipe (courtesy of Aberdeen City Libraries).

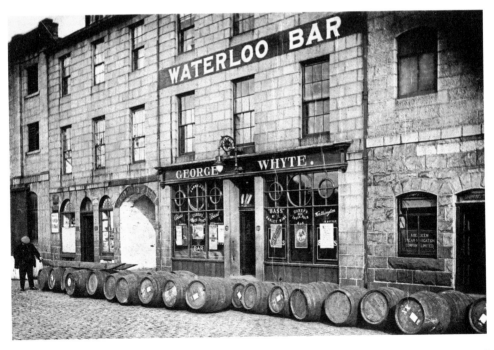

The Waterloo Bar at Waterloo Quay popular with fishermen and shipyard workers (courtesy of Aberdeen City Libraries).

What has not changed is the tendency to overindulge. In 1894 Alex Wilson, licensee of the Prince of Wales Hotel, was charged with selling drink to two men already very intoxicated from taking whiskies in the Lemon Tree and beer at Pirie's earlier. The pair had been turned away from Macandrew's before arriving in St Nicholas Lane where they were caught whisky in hand, as the police sergeant who tasted it confirmed, but it was the police who were ticked off by the magistrate for trying to tell the innkeeper who he could and could not provide with drink.

Tolerance of drunkenness waned with the nineteenth century as support for teetotalism grew. The famous Shiprow Tavern was a temperance house, not to be confused with the 1709 Ship Tavern at St Katherine's Court which was not, and whose name changed to the Workmen's Tavern, a favourite tippling-house with men from Shore Porters for its London porter (although Aberdeen porter was reputedly superior).

Around 8,000 Aberdonians signed the pledge to abstain from all intoxicating drinks, except as medicine or holy wine, but still when Aberdeen's Temperance Society founded in 1837 published a list of the city's licensed premises in the *Northern Temperance Record* it proved a long list. The teetotallers met weekly in their impressive hall in George Street

Thomson, Marshall's Aulton Brewery.

Above left: A fine grey and pink polished granite temperance fountain in Duthie Park.

Above right: Aberdeen evangelist warning of the perils of alcohol.

and among their successful conversions was Jamie Fraser, an overseer with Aberdeen Commercial Co., a big man with a capacity to consume alcohol to match his size – habitually downing 10 half-gills (nearly 3 litres) before breakfast. On signing the pledge he started up his own teetotal group from the Dogs and Monkey's Hall in the Gallowgate always crowded with seamen he called the Sons of Neptune.

Bath Temperance Hotel, later the Royal Hotel on Bath Street, was another popular spot. A different Royal Hotel on Union Street was run by the aforesaid prodigious businessman Isaac Machray, recognisable by his fiery face and temper. On summer evenings he hired militia bands to parade between his hotel at the corner of Union Street and Market Street (which retained the name Royal Buildings long after and was the site of Falconer's store) and the Castlegate. And pleasant it must have been enjoying Machray's hospitality in the long summer evenings as Bob Donaldson gave it gusto on his big drum.

Machray also ran mail and stagecoaches from his hotels so mornings could be as noisy with departing coaches, such as: the Union, Defiance, Duke of Richmond each with a set of four keen horse, or cattle as they were called, and Davy Troup, Tom Gray, John Rattray and the Cooks resplendent in red coats and white hats supervising the boarding of passengers – paying ones inside and the odd penniless soul on top with the luggage; some to endure the twenty-four hours overland to Edinburgh. When all was complete Howatt sounded the bugle for off.

Liquor laws were tightened during the nineteenth century: licences and hours of sales were restricted partly from the dangers of drunken workers operating machinery and partly the result of pressure from the temperance and Sabbatarian movements. Liquor sales licences were issued by magistrates for a fee of 2s and in 1830 there were some 870 licensed premises for Aberdeen's population of 60,000. By 1842 this number had dropped to 399, still an astonishing number for the size of the city. The Forbes Mackenzie Act of 1853 placed a curfew of 11.00 p.m. on bars with no Sunday opening. Rules were introduced regulating grocers selling alcohol and similar restrictions placed on taverns selling groceries. From 1901 children under fourteen years of age could only buy alcohol in quantities of less than one pint or in corked and sealed vessels while regulations restricted the sale of intoxicating liquor to those in charge of horses.

Aberdeen's Chief Constable Thomas Wyness was a rigorous implementer of liquor legislation during the late nineteenth century, hence his nickname the Terror of the Trade. His men disrupted back-of-shop (lock-in) drinking and encouraged licensees to remove internal partitions to create one large room that allowed bar staff to keep an eye on

A selection of Aberdeen brewers and a King's Highway nip glass.

Invoice from Bowman & Webster of South Constitution Street, Dundee and Seville (courtesy of Aberdeen City Libraries).

intoxicated customers, so reducing the number of bars offering the 'old treacle cask or cistern trick' of snugs where drunks could hide.

William Skene in his *East Neuk Chronicles* recounts the joke that public houses never opened because they never shut; alcohol was everywhere and readily available and the city's streets were full of inebriated individuals. When policing patrols were numbered in single figures these Charlies, as they were known, with their capes and blue Tam o' Shanter bonnets would scoop up a drunken body and wheel him or her by barrow (sprung from 1863 for greater comfort) to the watch-house to sober up.

Drinking tastes, if not habits, changed. Aberdeen's strong links with the continent ensured plentiful supplies of French wines in earlier centuries until import duties hiked up their prices. William Moyse's tavern in 1480 sold red Gascony wines for sixpence a Scotch pint. Four hundred years later ale was the main tipple, many local, some imported like a popular black beer from Danzig.

Brewers at Devanha included William Black & Coy whose popular table beers, porter and strong ale were exported as well as sold locally. Other public breweries included Lochside, Old Aberdeen, Holburn, King Street, Gilcomston, the Glenburnie at Rubislaw Den and the Ale Brewery on Virginia Street.

Jopp, wine and spirit merchants. James Jopp was the Lord Provost who presented Dr Johnson with the freedom of the town in August 1773.

Whisky only replaced claret as a popular drink once wines were priced beyond the pocket of most. Aberdeen produced little whisky but the countryside around was awash with the juice o' the barley with alert and crafty smugglers making frequent gruelling journeys across rough country, one step ahead of the gauger or excise man, their precious cargos secured to the backs of ponies. In Watty Reid's tavern, popular with tradesmen and the local militia, was inscribed over his fireplace:

> Fine Devanha porter; gweed strong ale;
> Real Cabrach whisky, as ever bore the bell.
> Watty's liquor's gweed;
> Gin ye hae nae money, Watty has nae trust.

It wasn't Burns but the message was clear. Sales were by cash only.

An innkeeper from Banchory swore by porter as good for a body so long as 'you don't take above a dozen.' He is possibly the same man who when informed that a heavy-drinking friend drowned when his timber raft came to grief near Crathes on the River Dee remarked, 'I am surprised at that, for I never kenn'd him to pass the inn before without coming in for a glass.'

In the seventeenth century a Cup o' Bon-Accord, 'ane silver cup, with the cover all dubill over gilt with gold,' and inscribed with the town's motto, *Bon-Accord* was filled with good claret and 'sweet confections' and offered to distinguished visitors to Aberdeen. This friendly welcome ended when some covenanting ministers declined the honour with no little embarrassment to the town but in a noble gesture the valuable Bon-Accord cup was presented to the fiery 'zealot' Andrew Cant, head of the Scottish covenanters as a gift to his church, St Nicholas, and was never seen again. This would not have endeared the preacher to that section of Aberdeen townsfolk who had 'pelted with stones and earth and a raven ... symbolic of evil' the unpopular Cant and his followers.

The New Inn frequently captured in illustrations of the Castlegate occupying the corner of Union and King Streets was later replaced by Archibald Simpson's North of Scotland Bank, in its turn now a public house; from whose portico roof the blue-robed figure of the Roman goddess Ceres gazes out serenely.

Built around 1755 by the Aberdeen Lodge of Freemasons the three-storey inn, its Masonic hall on its upper floor, dominated Castle Street. Hugely popular it offered roomy accommodation and its own post-chaise (small carriage for hire) along with plentiful stabling and carriage quarters, in what became known as Lodge Walk.

At a period when wealthy and poor lived cheek by jowl the New Inn accommodated both – royalty mingled with men and women from nearby poultry, flesh and meal markets and the graffiti on its glass windows scratched by diamond rings.

Dr Johnson and James Boswell stayed at the New Inn on their way to the Western Isles in 1773. Unwisely they had not booked ahead and the inn being full Boswell had to use his

The New Inn next to the Tolbooth and Town House in 1822.

celebrity to secure them beds for the night yet despite their hosts going to considerable lengths to accommodate them the surly doctor's jaundiced impression of Scotland remained. His appetite, however, was unaffected for he consumed several servings of Scotch barley broth with peas before declaring he would be in no hurry to have it again. Aberdeen and its friendly people did make an impression particularly the sight of the inn's maids who went about barefoot.

During his visit Dr Johnson was happy to be made a burgess of the city and happier still on discovering he was not expected to provide a tip for the tribute, as was the custom in England. As he paraded through the town with his burgess ticket pinned to his hat for all to admire Dr Johnson got 'plastered' while lingering too long to watch a harler at work in Huxter Row. Having waited in vain for the lexicographer to move on the workman eventually resumed his task unintentionally splashing the doctor with the gritty-lime contents of his pail.

In September 1787 it was the national bard Robert Burns' turn to tour the north. The Burns family originated from around Stonehive (Stonehaven) and Burns used the trip to meet with relatives during his stay at the New Inn. He also took the opportunity to discuss poetry with notables including Bishop Skinner and James Chalmers, editor of the *Aberdeen Journal*. Whether or not he slept in the same bed as Dr Johnson we shall never know.

Among the many clubs that met there was the Philosophical Society or the Wise Club mainly drawn from professors from Aberdeen's universities: King's and Marischal, including Thomas Reid and James Beattie. The Society also convened at John Beans and Lucky Campbell's in the Aulton (old town) although Beattie's preferred howff was in Luxembourg Close. Wise Club conversation flowed as liberally as the drink apparently – punch at a 2s 6d per Mutchken, port at 2s a 'botel' and porter besides. Tobacco 'paipes' were 6d each extra, as was the cost of entertainment bringing the total for an evening to around 3s each. The tragic death of Professor Ross of King's who choked to death on a spider in his glass of claret occurred after the break up of the group.

On a similarly gloomy note a drinking session between the lairds of Leith Hall and Mayen (Abernethy of Rothiemay) ended with Leith's death and Abernethy's flight abroad following their dual on the plainstones outside the New Inn:

> If brave Leith-Hall's been ta'en in drink,
> His sin's, I hope, forgiven;
> And I may safely say, this day,
> His soul is safe in heaven.

The last Stuart monarch to visit Aberdeen was James VII, the Old Pretender. On 23 December 1715 he stopped off at Skipper Scott's inn en route from Peterhead to Fetteresso Castle to be crowned. The coronation never took place but an old king that has survived is the Old King's Highway on the Green. There has been an inn there since medieval times when the Green was the main south road in and out of Aberdeen. As for the ancient fortified tower house once owned by Sir Robert Keith of Benholm, better known as the Wallace Tower, a bar was incorporated into it in 1895. In 1964 the Wallace Tower was removed to Tillydrone when the heart was ripped out of Aberdeen city centre in the name of progress.

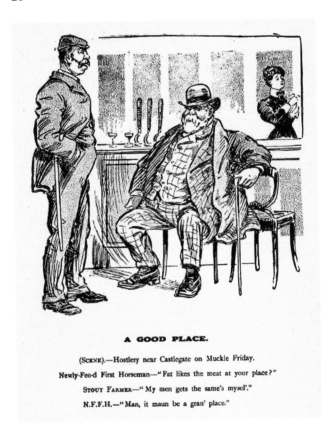

A GOOD PLACE.

(SCENE).—Hostlery near Castlegate on Muckle Friday.

Newly-Fee-d First Horseman—"Fat likes the meat at your place?"

STOUT FARMER—"My men gets the same's mysel'."

N.F.F.H.—"Man, it maun be a gran' place."

Left: Cartoon 'A Good Place' set in one of many bars around the Castlegate during Muckle Friday, the Feein' Market, when farmers and farm servants gathered six-monthly to hire and be hired.

Below: Dating from 1741 The Old King's Highway bar as it looks today.

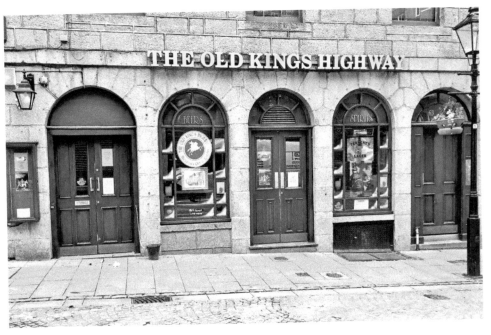

The Wallace Tower at the Wallace Nook (courtesy of Aberdeen City Libraries).

DID YOU KNOW?

Until the mid-nineteenth century when English imperial measures were imposed, Scotland's measures differed by area and variation from the yardstick Stirling jug. Aberdeen pints were greater than Stirling pints which were at least twice the quantity of English pints. A dent on the lip of Aberdeen's gauge pewter jug led to slightly smaller measures from the reign of James II.

The Hairy Bar, also known as the Aberdeen Arms and Murdo's, in West North Street got its name from the numerous stables in the vicinity which provided accommodation for coaches, carters, riders and their horses. King Street's Capital Inn, for example, accommodated eight carriages and forty horses. Horse hair was collected from stables and sold for stuffing mattresses.

Aberdonian tailor William Watson who stitched Lord Byron's first pair of breeks was also a poet who fed up listening to renderings of 'The Roast Beef of Old England' from an English regiment garrisoned at Aberdeen during the American War of Independence would lustily counter with verses from his own humorous patriotic song 'The Kail Brose of Scotland'.

3. The Gassy Gordons

In the summer of 1824 a notice in the *Aberdeen Journal* had people flocking to a meeting in the New Inn; a proposal to manufacture gas in the city hoped to attract investors ... it succeeded ... Aberdeen's first oil and gas boom was underway and within weeks a large gasometer was erected.

A good return on the speculation looked guaranteed. The city's population was growing fast, from 27,000 in 1801 to 45,000 twenty years on, straining basic civic amenities including street lighting. Then there was the innovation made by Aberdeen's Broadford Works – the first industrial premises in Scotland lit by gas. Boulton and Watt, employers of Scotsman William Murdoch who recognised the potential of distilling gas to light homes, factories and streets had installed gas lighting into Broadford's in 1814. It is against this background so many were prepared to sink their savings into the Aberdeen Gas Light Co. at Poynernook.

The appeal of gas for homes and industry is easy to appreciate; an efficient fuel to replace smelly whale oil lamps and the six-penny candle for lighting.

Gibb & Hay Lithographers to Her Majesty, Aberdeen

CASTLE STREET.

In 1824 speculators flocked to the New Inn (on the right of the picture) to invest in gas manufacture in Aberdeen.

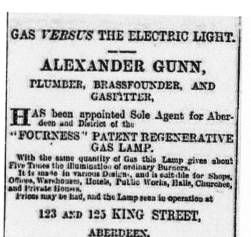
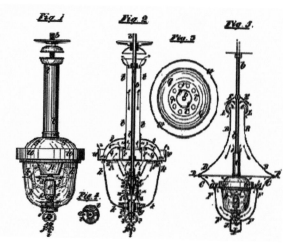

Advertisement for gas lamps, 1886.

Initially Poynernook's Gas Lane works manufactured an expensive olefiant gas, the UK's and possibly the world's first oil gas plant. As its name suggests this was an oil derivative produced by passing an iron tube through a hot coal furnace with air going in one end and the other submerged into a tank of oil. The gas generated delivered brilliant white light but its manufacture was so costly it was dropped after four years for the cheaper alternative of coal gas.

Shops, churches, schools, public buildings, businesses and homes as well as street lamps were converted to gas and in the nine years between 1832 and 1841 Aberdeen's gas consumption trebled, encouraging the emergence of a rival.

In 1844 the rather unimaginatively named New Gas Light Co. began production at Sandilands where previously aromatic herbs had grown. Two years of fierce competition brought lower tariffs for customers but squeezed profits and when the two firms amalgamated in 1846 prices again increased.

With gas production now concentrated at Sandilands an offshoot industry recycling its by-products was started up in 1848. John Miller's Chemical Works known as Stinky Miller's took its water from a 400-foot Artesian well which yielded the purest substance in the whole of the 5-acre site.

Aromatic herbs were now a distant memory. Noxious and often dangerous materials including tar, ammonia, creosote oil, sulphur, benzole (benzene) and naphtha were converted into a myriad of industrial and pharmaceutical uses and the company soon branched out into manufacturing fertilisers, some simply crushed bones, others chemical concoctions. Miller's began buying sulphuric acid from Richards & Co. linen manufacturer at Broadford Mills but the quantity proved insufficient and an acid plant was built at Sandilands which converted naphtha into sulphate of ammonia and dissolved bones. Paraffin wax was purified from coal and shale while phosphate rock, imported from the Pacific Islands and Russia, was turned into phosphoric acid. Miller's manufactured superphosphate fertilisers, which looked nothing like the traditional blood

Wapping Street was demolished for redevelopment around Mutton Brae and this former gas office was rebuilt at the corner of Mount Street and Westburn Road. The tablet on the architrave once bore the motto *Ex fumo dare lucem* (to give light from smoke).

and bone manures local farmers were used to, leading to complaints that Miller's bones were a 'stanes'. Farmers did still recognise Miller's fishmeal made from pulped fish bones, heads and guts supplied by Aberdeen's huge fishing industry and sought after by both agriculturists and horticulturists. With Miller's increasing dependency on science to create fertilisers the old practice and income source for Aberdeen's poorest selling their human waste for manure was brought to an end.

Stinky Miller's output tested the patience of generations of Aberdonians with its distinctive reek clinging to the city on the warmest of days. Unpleasant as that was it was nothing compared with the hazards faced by the workforce, the least of which was a tendency for rats to run up trouser legs when fish offal was disturbed. Hazardous and foul-smelling it might have been for its labourers but Miller's workforce was loyal with sons eager to follow their fathers into the trade.

Aberdeen's gas streetlamps were lit and extinguished initially by the city's night police or watchmen partly because they had so little to do after dark. The arrangement worked well until it came to the notice of a police Chief Constable elsewhere in Scotland who thought the practice diminished the force. Lamp lighting, he insisted, was not a police duty and so from 1875 dedicated lamplighters were employed.

In the 1860s as civil war raged in America gas consumers in Aberdeen were raging at the high cost of their gas compared with elsewhere in Britain. A defiant gas company listed

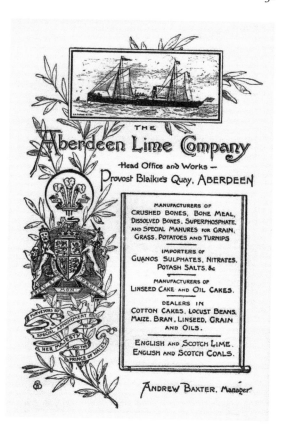

Right: Advertisement for Aberdeen Lime Co.

Below: Gas lamp beside Prince Albert Statue, then at Union Street and Union Terrace.

its reasons for high prices – Aberdeen gas was of better quality than any English town gas; the sprawling geography of the city required extensive networks of underground gas piping; distance from coalfields increased transport costs.

The cost of Aberdeen gas came up at a meeting in the Music Hall on 5 March 1862 to gauge public support for a council takeover of gas production; municipalization was a local authority equivalent of nationalisation. The big attendance demonstrated Aberdonians had lost none of their enthusiasm for gas with most in favour of the scheme and confident that council gas might prove cheaper than from a private company manufacturing gas for profit. There was also the hope that any money made on municipal gas would be put towards improving civic amenities although one audience member disagreed, stating, 'every tub (should) stand on its own bottom'.

Municipalization agreed, the Corporation Gas Works took over a site behind Cotton Street, between the Links and Miller Street, in 1871 and George Gordon, former manager of the old company, was paid compensation of £2,000. The transfer of his business to the city cost £6,000, around £4 million today, but it did result in lower prices for customers and improved conditions of employment for gas workers; their hours were reduced from twelve to eight with greater free time than their previous entitlement of one full day off in six weeks. The exhausting, dangerous work in temperatures up to 130 degrees Fahrenheit could not be eliminated entirely but the worst exploitation with the practice of employing old men to break up blocks of coal with hammers for a paltry five pennies per ton (although a welcome source of income before the introduction of old age pensions) was tackled and long gone.

For the 200 gas works' employees and 100 men and boys at Stinky Miller's work was inherently perilous with toxic fumes, chemical spills, explosions and fire hazards. When William Murray was killed at the gas works in 1904 his widow received a weekly allowance of 12s and sixpence for a period of six years. Such was the sense of community and recognition of the importance of those industries to the economy that when a huge fire broke out at the Sandilands works the Provost and councillors were among volunteers rushing to help tackle it. Injuries and deaths were regrettably not unusual before the introduction of health and safety legislation and the growing popularity of gas was accompanied by increasing casualties from among the general public often out of ignorance and carelessness.

In 1866 a blast under the floor of the cutting-room at Marshall & Co. in Jopp's Lane left four seriously injured young women, one of whom later died, following a gas leak in the underground drainage system. When an explosion lifted the entire roof off a house on Holburn Street it landed back more or less in situ while stones 'heavy enough to have killed an elephant' flew through the air and onto the street.

Fate intervened when a workman was repairing an electric clock outside premises on George Street at the same time a group of men were delivering an automatic piano to Humber's Waxworks close by and below street level telephone cables were being laid. The cabler punctured a gas pipe at the moment a piano mover stepped onto a manhole cover and the clock repairer switched on the electric current. The manhole cover flew into the air and flames shot skyward from the hole. A man and a boy were flung into the street but escaped major injuries.

Above left: Aberdeen Corporation Gas showroom at Broad Street and Union Street.

Above right: Gas 'Electrolux' refrigerators claimed to never wear out, promoted by Aberdeen Gas.

In a similar incident a culvert was blown 20 feet into the air at the junction of Union Street and Broad Street. It was busy at midday and the resulting fire and flying debris created panic and cut off electricity supplies. The blast plunged a lift in nearby Crown Mansions into darkness and it jolted to a stop with passengers fearing they were about to plunge to their deaths but were eventually able to crawl out to safety.

When Mrs Sim, a carter's wife from Stevenson Street, struck a match to see if she had a gas leak in her meter cupboard she and her children were lucky to escape the resulting fire. Less fortunate was the family of Frederick McKinnon of the well-known engineering company. His wife was at home in View Terrace with their twenty-month-old daughter Helen Blanche and the child's nursemaid when she smelled gas. Mrs McKinnon immediately opened a window but then went to light the gasalier in the sitting room with a lighted taper. She was blown out of the room along with the maid who was holding the baby. A door slammed shut, amputating part of the child's arm. They all suffered burns and were treated on the spot by Dr Alexander Ogston, a prominent anaesthetist at the infirmary and close neighbour from Rosemount Place, who in a twist of coincidence was the inventor of a chloroform gas mask.

The convenience of gas overcame many concerns with its safety but for the domestic customer its cost and the expense of appliances restricted its use until the council set up a leasing service. At the beginning of the twentieth century it was hiring out 2,000 stoves and 400 gas fires in addition to grills, boiler rings and other gas equipment.

Budgeting was also helped with the introduction of pre-payment meters but a crime wave accompanied their installation with thieves stealing cash from them. In 1906 three men were jailed for theft from a penny-in-the-slot gas meter and a nineteen year old was sentenced to three months for stealing 4p from another meter. Opportunities were plentiful for such petty-theft with over 6,000 homes in Aberdeen with slot meters in addition to 32,000 ordinary meters.

Gas marketing exhibitions attracted large crowds. In 1906 in the Music Hall a 'glittering extravaganza' featuring a lamp equivalent to 1,000 candles and a flash-light advertising sign for Lawson, Turnbull & Co. drew such enormous crowds that the event was extended by several days. Aberdeen's gas consumption rocketed from around 9 million cubic feet in 1832 to 600 million by 1906. Over the same period prices plummeted from Aberdeen Gas Light Co.'s initial charge of 40s per cubic foot to under 3s for council gas by 1900.

In 1887 Aberdeen Harbour Board gave permission for the council to transport cargoes of coal to its Cotton Street gas works by steam locomotives instead of horse-drawn wagons. The familiar wee steam engines running to and from the harbour became well-loved attractions: *City of Aberdeen, Bon-Accord* and the slightly less glamorously named *Aberdeen Gas Works No. 3* – painted in Aberdeen Corporation green. With UK-wide nationalisation of gas in 1949 Aberdeen's little gas railway became the property of the Scottish Gas Board and one of the engines was named after its marketing symbol, *Mr Therm*.

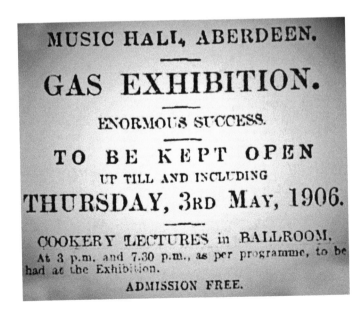

Newspaper notice of Gas Exhibition in the Music Hall, 1906.

Former Aberdeen Corporation Gas locomotive *Mr Therm* at Seaton Park.

Of the little collier vessels which made up the fleet bringing in coal supplies to Aberdeen the *Firth* is perhaps best known; launched from Hall, Russell's yard in 1908 she was sunk in July 1915 by a German U-boat during the First World War.

There is symmetry to Aberdeen's gas industries. What began with oil in 1824 resorted to coal and in the 1970s an oil reforming plant replaced coal at Miller Street. As the industry faced stiff competition from electricity North Sea oil came on stream and 150 years after Aberdeen's first gas production at Poynernook a new gas revolution came to Aberdeen.

Did You Know?

The Gordon family who ran the gas company were known as the Gassy Gordons.

In 1870, one year before taking over manufacturing and supplying town gas, Aberdeen Corporation pledged to supply citizens with gas lights of the intensity of twenty-five sperm whale oil candles weighing six to the pound burning at 120 grains per minute.

Gas streetlamps continued well into the twentieth century with Union Street's operating in tandem with electric lights which were turned off at 10.30 p.m. when gas ones were lit.

Former gas steam loco, *Mr Therm*, is now in the children's area of Seaton Park. You can ride on a train pulled by *Bon-Accord* at the Royal Deeside Railway at Crathes while over the hill on Donside locomotive *No. 3* resides at Grampian Transport Museum in Alford and the *City of Aberdeen* locomotive is now in the hands of the Scottish Railway Preservation Society.

4. And Scalding Tears Pour Down of Boiling Lead

The Church of St Nicholas, Aberdeen's Mither Kirk, which according to the historian William Robbie was 'acknowledged to be one of the finest parish churches in Scotland' and has dominated life in the city for over 1,000 years was very nearly lost one night in 1874 when it became engulfed in flames.

It might be more accurate to refer to the kirks of St Nicholas for it had split into East and West churches at the Reformation with both halves undergoing alterations and restoration before and after which obliterated all but scant remains of the original beneath hints of Gothic, touches of Norman and much else besides. The name abides, St Nicholas, patron saint of mariners. St Nicholas, in some form or another, has witnessed all kinds of upheavals from the Wars of Independence to Piper Alpha. Robert the Bruce and his family worshipped here. His sister Christian lived locally and presented St Nicholas with a silver chalice studded with precious stones, sadly it went missing. When the English garrison was routed from Dunnottar Castle following the successful use of the rallying cry, *Bon-Accord*, those not spared as currency to be exchanged for Bruce's sister, being held for ransom by the English king, were buried in the kirk's graveyard. Prior to the Battle of Otterburn in 1388 the Scottish parliament met in Aberdeen and its barons' prayers in the kirk were on that occasion heeded. Mary, sister of Scotland's first

St Nicholas Kirk's oak steeple before the fire (courtesy of Aberdeen City Libraries).

East and West churches with the new spire in position.

portrait painter George Jamesone, presented tapestries to the church which survive today.

The tall granite spire of St Nicholas with its distinctive pinnacles dominating the city centre is relatively recent and the consequence of the disastrous fire of Friday 9 October 1874 which destroyed the old square oak tower and its renowned peal of bells. The blazing steeple was said to have, 'roared like a huge blast furnace' before lurching to one side and crashing to the ground.

> Hark! from the steeple chimes the deep-voiced bell,
> Thundering those iron tones we love so well

Imagine the despair and horror etched into the faces of assembled Aberdonians drawn to the scene by the noise, flames, smoke and reek of their kirk ablaze. Imagine the great racket of its magnificent bells melting in the intense heat, discordantly tolling as they plunged to earth – Lawrence, Big Lowrie, a giant of bells lost forever. The steeple clock made for 200 merks by John Kray of Crail, familiar to generations of Aberdonians making their way to and from work or casually glancing up at it when passing or checking they were in time for worship – reduced to smithereens. Centuries-old seasoned timbers cracking and roaring, consumed by flames, breaking free from their joists and nails and toppling as charred waste. The steeple's lead sheath reduced to bubbling liquid that dripped as rivulets then lethal torrents pouring down; it must have appeared like a vision out of Hell. Certainly one or two of the Kirk's more pious followers feared the night's destruction signified the portentous 'burning of kirks.'

> And scalding tears pour down of boiling lead

The cause of the fire was more prosaic. The church was lit by gas fed through open jets called Sunlights. It is thought a lamp had not been extinguished and the water-cooling reservoir beneath the burners had dried out. Puffs of smoke were seen that evening escaping from the tower followed by 'little jets of flame' and shortly after the steeple separating East and West churches at Drum's and Collison's aisles was consumed by fire.

St Nicholas Kirk is home to the UK's largest carillon of bells. Bells have traditionally been big in the city. From 1351, the year the Black Death finally released its grip on Europe, until the Reformation the tolling of Big Lowrie marked important events. And in later times Lowrie struck 4.00 a.m. to rouse Aberdonians from sleep at the start of the working day. The church's minor bells chimed the quarter hours and Lowry's little sister, Maria, rang for prayers. Lowrie and Maria had been presented to the church by Aberdeen's provost William de Leith as way of penance for having killed Baillie Cattenach during a quarrel at the Barkmill, by the West burn. Three centuries of tolling rendered the bells in need of attention and both were recast in Flanders in the seventeenth century when Lowrie was inscribed by the restorer:

Soli Deo gloria – Michael Burgerhaus me fecit, Anno Domini 1634
(To God alone be the glory – Michael Burgerhaus hath made me,
in the year of the Lord 1634)

Engraving of the disastrous fire showing firemen and volunteers on the roof of the West Kirk of St Nicholas desperately trying to save it and the steeple (courtesy of Aberdeen City Libraries).

The steeple destroyed in the fire had been part of a 1750s restoration when the West church, then a ruin, was reinstated from designs drawn up by the architect James Gibbs, an Aberdonian living in London, who died before work started. A plan to use Rubislaw granite was dropped in favour of Fifeshire sandstone, possibly on grounds of cost which was considerable. The roof lead, mainly from Leith plus scraps leftover from repairs to King's College in Old Aberdeen came to £600, substantially more than the cost of the lead on the earlier steeple acquired from England in exchange for salmon. The new steeple extended to 140 feet above the ground and was topped off with a gilt ball and weathercock. A local craftsman was commissioned to provide a replacement four-sided clock, not only decorative but functional at a period when few owned clocks and pocket watches.

It was mainly the East church rebuilt by Archibald Simpson in 1837 which was destroyed in the fire of 1874 along with the steeple and transepts. People of Aberdeen were deeply affected by the loss and its dramatic nature. Had the local fire brigade been more efficient the destruction may not have been as complete but confusion reigned, fire hoses leaked and the water supply proved inadequate for the might of the inferno.

The alarm was raised at a quarter past eight that Friday evening yet it was after nine before the first water was trained on the fire. Panic sums up the response when

The Mither Kirk, showing John Smith's colonnade. Note the missing spire following the fire of 1874 (courtesy of Aberdeen City Libraries).

no watercocks were found nearby so that fire hoses had to be laboriously trailed over rooftops from water mains some distance away.

Water might be in short supply but volunteers came hurrying to risk their lives to save the kirk. The fire brigade, men of the 36th Brigade Depot, were assisted by the ship crew of HM *Clyde* and militiamen and a fire engine from the barracks. Ordinary citizens who risked their lives to save the church were derisorily described as a mob by Baillie Esslemont. Two of the mob were Booth and Sandison who selflessly entered the burning steeple to clear fire hoses and their courage was rewarded with a paltry 20s as compensation for their burnt clothing. Another, William Keith Jnr, of King Street Granite Works, got his feet tangled in the confusion of hoses running through the steeple as he struggled to contain the fire and fell to his death.

> Who, on the ladder, in the fierce pell-mell
> Climbed as a man, but as a hero fell

The Northern Assurance Co. with whom the church was insured was highly critical of the response to the fire: insufficiency and delays in applying water; too few fire engines, water buckets and ladders; the state of fire hoses; lack of leadership. The council was singled out for special criticism for its unpreparedness for such an event.

When plans were drawn up to replace the lost steeple the authority was grudging in providing funds to adequately rebuild and so inflamed the fury of citizens. The press

Aberdeen Fire Brigade in 1875 in their 'uniform' of helmet and belt (courtesy of Aberdeen City Libraries).

On the extreme left of the drawing is where St Nicholas Kirk's insurer, Northern Insurance Company, established its offices (Monkey House) following their transfer from Doo-cot brae, lost when Union Street and Union Bridge were built (courtesy of Aberdeen City Libraries).

joined in, demanding the council recognise the importance to the city of this landmark building and to 'loosen the purse strings.'

> O infant Phoenix, what thou yet shalt be;
> But let Devana spare not time nor cost,
> Till thou shalt be more than thou ever wast.

William Smith, son of John Smith the notable city architect whose colonnade screens the kirk, ensured his design for the replacement church was in sympathy with Simpson's 1837 building while making the new spire above Collison's Aisle his own.

The replacement of the carillon within the new spire created a further row when the council insisted new bells should hang not in the new St Nicholas steeple but in the tower of the Municipal Buildings next to the Town House. There were accusations of it behaving *ultra vires* (committing an illegal act) of kirk plunder and the town's magistrates were dubbed hypocrites for acting disgracefully while sitting in judgement of others accused of lesser crimes. Quite some ding-dong you might say, which was presented as a conflict between church and community.

In the end the kirk was repaired and a taller, more slender steeple built. It still carries a four-face clock and with its thirty-six bells increased to forty-eight it retains its place as

The Donaldson Rose Bell prior to being raised to the carillon, 1887 (courtesy of Aberdeen City Libraries).

the largest carillon in the UK. Some of the bells were bought through public donations and some donated as private gifts.

In 1887 the arrival of the new bells from Belgium created great excitement and they were paraded through the streets from the railway station to St Nicholas Kirk. The new largest bell was a 3-tonner called Victoria, after the queen and not a saint, on whose jubilee it was first rung officially in 1887.

(Verse: Duncan MacGregor; *The Mystery Explained*: *How the East Kirk Took Fire*, 1874.)

Did You Know?

St Nicholas Kirk has the most medieval effigies of any Scottish parish church. It was a tradition in Aberdeen to celebrate the Feast of St Nicholas each 6 December.

During the Reformation all furnishings and ornamental carvings were removed from the church and people had to bring their own seats when attending sermons.

5. The World Begins at Spring Garden

Centuries before North Sea Oil and Gas established Aberdeen as a centre of offshore expertise and its skilled workforce a highly-prized global resource the city had already secured a reputation for innovation and quality. For sake of space this will be a mere snapshot of why.

Among the vast array of trades most practised in Aberdeen at one time or another were ship-building, granite, textiles, paper-making, comb-making and engineering. Problems relating to construction, industrial processing and manufacturing in the far corners of the world were often resolved in the Granite City.

William MacKinnon was just twenty-one years old when in 1798 he set up an iron foundry at Windy Wynd in Spring Garden. William MacKinnon & Co., Iron Founders and Engineers made its mark supplying specialised machinery to the immense British Empire for processing foodstuffs such as coffee, tea, rice and cacao and for the heavier, dirtier industries of diamond and tin mining. The company had branches in Nairobi and Salvador including outlets in sixty countries. Its catalogues, printed in four languages, illustrate both the scope of its equipment and extent of its markets in Burma, Malaya, Dutch Guiana,

Advertisement for a MacKinnon rice mill.

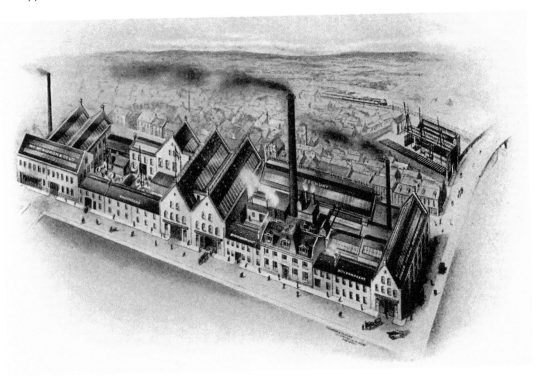

William MacKinnon & Co., ironfounders and engineers, Spring Garden.

MacKinnon's machinery was important to the development of the chocolate industries.

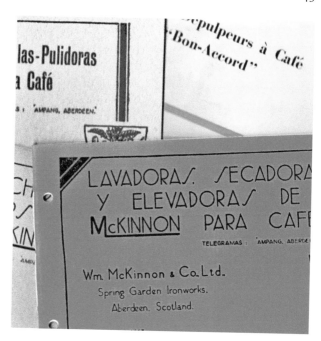

MacKinnon's international catalogues were published in several languages.

Columbia, Salvador, East and West Indies, French West Africa and all points east and west; MacKinnon's order books provide a lesson in economic and political geography.

Although 90 per cent of its output was exported overseas MacKinnon's dealt locally as well: many of Aberdeen's lampposts, manhole covers and drain branders were cast at Spring Garden and its high-quality tools and equipment were sought after for farming and horticulture both here and abroad.

It was not all plaudits for MacKinnon's. During the First World War the company was suspected of manufacturing defective ammunition shells with evidence emerging during an investigation and court case of secret meetings between the Director of Munitions in Scotland, Aberdeen's Lord Provost Taggart and MacKinnon's manager. As a consequence the company was put under state management for the duration of the war and run as a National Shell Factory. MacKinnon's manager was told, 'If this had been done in France you would have been stuck up against a wall and shot.' He was not shot but he left the company and it subsequently regained its fine reputation.

McKinnon's cast-iron went into building bridges, the old Strathspey railway bridge at Ballindalloch for example, but bridges were a mere sideline for McKinnon. Think Aberdeen bridges and the name that springs to mind is Harper.

John Harper from Turriff began work at nine years of age as an apprentice market gardener but when he moved away from the Northeast he found work as a fencer and so began his fascination with wire. By the mid-1850s John and his brother Hugh were living in Aberdeen where they added to the city's several iron foundries. However, as Harper & Co., Iron Gate and Wire Manufacturers, they did well producing and supplying fencing for Scotland's farms and estates where drystane dykes were not used and for fencing off stretches of the Great North of Scotland Railway – and abroad too, for the Great Indian

Left: Preserved gateway on Gerrard Street that once led into MacKinnon's.

Below: Louis Harper designed the Craiginches Ironworks for his father John, 1892.

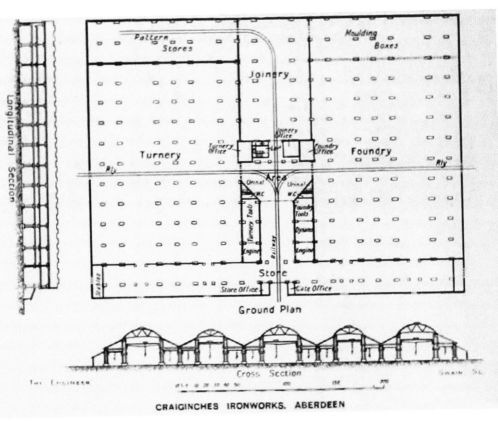

CRAIGINCHES IRONWORKS, ABERDEEN

Peninsula Railway. In 1863 the company patented a gearing system for tensioning wire, for fencing certainly, but equally effective on suspension bridges.

Following the Torry ferryboat disaster in 1876 John Harper offered to provide a wire footbridge to connect Aberdeen with Torry on 'liberal terms' – payment of a half-penny each crossing for one year. His offer was rejected when it was decided to build a larger granite bridge instead and Harper shifted his focus beyond Aberdeen, to Kathmandu and Estonia, to the West Indies and the Falkland Islands. Harper's could easily claim to have bridged the world and left their name stamped on each tensioning post as proof of quality.

J. M. Henderson & Co. Ltd not-so-long-ago a major engineering employer in the city, started out in a small way at Jopp's Lane in 1866. Early success prompted a move into larger premises on King Street by 1878.

When granite quarry owner John Fyfe saw a cable stretched across the river at Abergeldie to allow mail be passed from one side to the other he realised a similar system could be applied on a larger scale to his quarry at Kemnay for moving stone greater distances than was possible by crane. He turned to Henderson to build the ropeways which came to be known as blondins after the famous tightrope walker and were adopted by quarries everywhere.

In addition Henderson & Co. built and supplied equipment for all manner of large-scale working: gold fields in the Klondike; phosphate beds in the Pacific Islands; sugar estates in the West Indies; dock yards in Turkey; water works in Australia; construction plants in

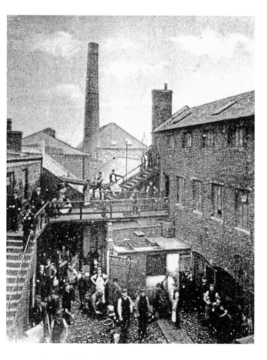

Above left: Blaikie & Sons, Footdee: braziers, bell and brass founders, plumbers, gas-fitters, coppersmiths and everything metal. James and Thomas Blaikie became Lord Provosts of Aberdeen.

Above right: 'Most dams start in Aberdeen' claims an advertisement for J. M. Henderson cableways.

J. M. Henderson cableways used in construction of the Naga Hamadi Barrage on the River Nile in Upper Egypt.

New Zealand; South Africa; Finland; India ... stick a pin in an atlas and it's likely you will strike a place that dealt with Henderson.

A glimpse at Henderson's catalogues illustrates the scope of their phenomenal global success: hydro-electric dams and barrages from Loch Ericht to Iraq; canals in Holland; naval bases from the Scapa Flow to Singapore; bridges from Uganda to Rio. Henderson invented and manufactured plant to suit the needs of heavy industries – aerial cableways, dragline excavators, drag scrapers and cranes.

Cranes were a Henderson speciality: travelling; dock-side; tower; jib; grabbing and derrick ranging from 3-ton tiddlers to 32-ton giants for building the Forth Road Bridge.

As with most heavy engineering works Henderson diversified into military output in war-time: Howitzers, Bailey bridges, mine sweeping gear, components for shells and tanks, ammunition hoists etc.

On a different scale but equally global was Aberdeen's long lost comb industry. Vast cargoes of horn and bone shipped across oceans or piled onto carts from the city's slaughterhouses – 100,000 pieces of horn each week; buffalo hooves, tortoiseshell, whalebone, cattle bones and for variety, exotic woods – delivered to Aberdeen combmakers; one-man businesses initially later concentrated into a single company. Yes, Aberdeen was once the comb manufacturing centre of the world, producing nine million plain and decorated items comprising 2,000 different designs at its height. No nineteenth-century mahogany dressing table was complete without a beautifully crafted Aberdeen comb to dress society women's elaborates hair styles. Many a man's beard was tamed by running an Aberdeen comb through it. Cheaper and plainer combs made their way into the humblest kitchen drawer in the far reaches of the world. Specialist combs designed for West African hair and gilded ones for India. At the peak of the

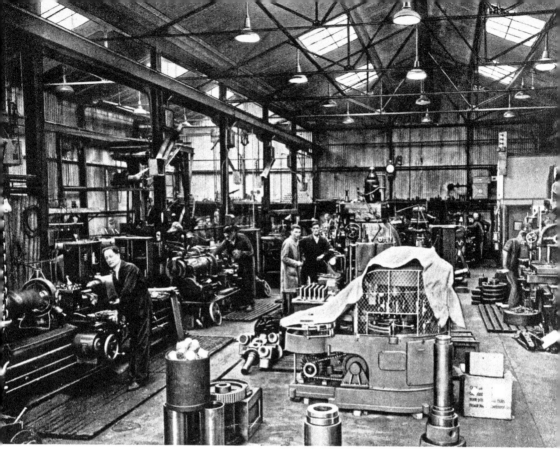

J. M. Henderson machine shop, 1940s.

trade 50 per cent of the total UK imports of ox horn went to Aberdeen's horner trade. A visitor to Aberdeen in 1851 found untidy piles of imported horn littered both harbour and Combworks, often exotic, sometimes enormous, from the East Indies, Siam, South America and the Cape of Good Hope.

Founded in 1830 Stewart, Rowell & Co. grew, absorbed smaller businesses, and by the end of the nineteenth century was winning medals for its outstanding products at exhibitions in London, Vienna, Sydney, Adelaide, Melbourne, Antwerp, Chicago and Paris.

Combs are plastic products meaning they are malleable and horn and bone are natural plastics. Early combs were cut by hand and later ones were heated and softened and the bone pressed into moulds and machine cut. Tortoiseshell was pretty but expensive and cheaper alternatives for the mass market were made from bone yellowed by soaking it in diluted nitric acid then neutralised in a mixture of red lead oxide which created tortoiseshell-like orange tints – a process carried out by women and girls. Once sawn, washed, dried, polished and buffed with wheels wrapped with walrus skin the imitation tortoiseshell was ready to be packed into boxes or stitched to cards for displaying in shops.

Nothing went to waste. Scraps and scrapes discarded by comb-makers were blended for knife and umbrella handles or made into prussiate of potash; a lemon coloured chemical sold to confectioners for its pineapple flavour.

Aberdeen Combworks advertisement.

Mechanisation made combs cheaper. A 50 horse-power steam engine, 'the largest of the horizontal kind in Scotland' could produce 2,000 combs for every 100 crafted by hand and despite eleven separate processes involved in making women's side-combs they sold for only 1p per pair in the 1860s.

At the height of its success in the nineteenth century Aberdeen Combworks employed some 1,000 men, women, girls and boys, four times the number of horners across the whole of the rest of Scotland combined. The work was hot, deafeningly noisy, foul-smelling and highly dangerous in an atmosphere thick with bone dust and machines potentially lethal for operatives. There was a 300-ton heavy-duty hydraulic press used to apply decorations, break down horn fibres and expand bone; grinders; machines like giant nut crackers with steel dies for engraving; mechanical chisels and saws large and delicate. Accidents were common and in March 1849 a girl's back was broken when she was dragged into a machine.

When competition from synthetic materials such as the rubber composite Vulcanite and celluloid threatened Aberdeen's supremacy in comb production the Combworks hit back with its own version of celluloid. Keronyx which could be manufactured in a dazzling array of colours as well as imitation tortoiseshell and rhinoceros was a derivative of milk and the waste from its production went into making an agricultural fertiliser called Keronikon which was marketed overseas.

Unusual aerial view of Aberdeen Combworks from a balloon on a misty day.

Besides combs, Aberdeen's Combworks produce just about everything once associated with horn – spoons, beakers, scoops, fruit knives, boxes, shoehorns, paper-knives, bagpipe mouthpieces – its success translated into branches in London and Birmingham.

The beauty and glamour of much of the output from the Combworks belied their dangerous and unhealthy origins and those maimed and killed in their manufacture are not commemorated by statues honouring their sacrifice. However, in a corner of St Peter's cemetery on King Street stands a once impressive though now crumbling granite tombstone marking the grave of John McPherson, an independent combmaker, later with Stewart Combworks, who along with his brother James was active in the Chartist movement which called for extending democracy and workers' rights in Britain.

Aberdeen, tucked into the Northeast coast of Scotland, has punched beyond its size for industrial innovation with many more examples than I have space for here.

Aberdeen was one of Britain's major textile manufacturing centres with nearly a quarter of the town's population employed in the trade during the 1830s. Scotland's hosiery industry began in Aberdeen in the eighteenth century as a cottage industry with locally-grown flax spun into linen thread then woven into cloth. After flax came wool.

James Hadden initially worked a put-out system supplying wool to women in and around Aberdeen who would knit it into stockings and mitts which were exchanged by Hadden's men for more wool and the finished garments packaged and dispatched from Aberdeen. With innovations in machinery designed to speed up textile production people came to be employed in the manufactory or mill and Hadden's mill at the foot of

Tombstone of John McPherson, combmaker and Chartist, in St Peter's graveyard.

Windmill Brae grew into a huge enterprise. From stockings as fine as could be pulled through a finger ring to quality worsted carpets, from the famous Aberdeen Wincey (a blend of linen and cotton) to rougher fabrics – the city on the export labels read Aberdeen and brought immense fortunes to local textile manufacturers.

The name Crombie long associated with the luxury end of textiles started as Knowles and Crombie early in the nineteenth century, at Cothal Mills. By 1828 it was simply Crombie and expansion took them to Grandholm. Crombie's boast was it would go to any length to fulfil orders: running a naval blockade to deliver rebel Confederate officers' grey uniforms during the American Civil War and during the Franco-Prussian War an order of cloth was flown into besieged Paris by balloon. Thomas Blake Glover was an agent in Japan, among other things, for this company that produced the British army greatcoat, an icon of the First World War. Its other overcoats warmed the backs of Russian leaders from Tsars to Gorbachev and its cloth was fashioned into garments for celebrities from Cary Grant to the Beatles.

Rough materials such as flax canvas for ship sails, seamless water hoses, mail bags and linoleum-backing were manufactured in appalling conditions by hundreds of children, men and women at Richards' Broadford jute works, Scotland's oldest iron-framed mill and the country's first industrial plant to have gas lighting installed.

Farquhar and Gill Ltd were established in 1818 making it one of the earliest paint manufacturers in the UK. It marketed the first ready-mixed paint and under the name Fargil it supplied its enamel paint to the Admiralty for its ships. As part of its global reach

Drawing of Windmill Brae with cast-iron pillar fountain on extreme right and Hadden's textile mill in the background dominating the Green.

The colour shop at Farquhar & Gill's extensive premises, St Paul's Street.

Fargil operated offices in Canada, South Africa and New Zealand as well as throughout Britain and Ireland.

Look down and you may see the words Aberdeen Adamant beneath your feet. The Adamant Stone & Paving Co. Ltd of 1885 took granite chips from Dancing Cairns quarry, mixed them with concrete and compressed them into paving stones they called Adamant, from the Greek *adamas* meaning rigid or invincible. You could be anywhere in Britain and find yourself on a little piece of Aberdeen.

Paper has been manufactured in and around Aberdeen since Patrick Sandilands of Cotton established a mill at Gordon's Mills in 1696. As recently as forty years ago five paper mills operated around Aberdeen producing paper for every purpose, from potato sacks to colour-tinted fine writing paper. Davidson's of Mugiemoss boasted the largest board machine in Scotland and was the leading producer of paper bags in the UK. Paper for bank notes used to be manufactured at Inverurie's Tait's mill while Pirie's has won

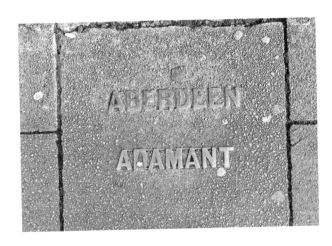

Left: Aberdeen Adamant paving slabs on Holburn Street.

Below: Alex Pirie & Sons 35-acre Stoneywood Works.

the highest awards for the excellence of its fine writing and book papers, its innovative watermarks and embossed products. Interestingly Pirie's created a near self-sufficient village at Stoneywood providing its workers and their families with a school, library and playing fields. As Pirie Appleton and Co. in College Street they became one of the largest manufacturers of stationary in the world and introduced the River Series envelopes which are still with us today along with the self-seal envelope.

Aberdeen remains a centre of excellence and innovation but too many of its former industries have moved to other parts of Britain and overseas.

Alex Pirie Paper Manufacturer.

Did You Know?

In the early nineteenth century Aberdeen built more ships than any other British city and was renowned for her clippers which dominated Chinese and Australian trade while her coastal steamers operated from Shetland to London.

In the 1890s around 3,000 vessels shipped 700,000 tons of goods through the harbour, including exports of soft fruit from the 145 acres of strawberries grown in and around the city.

The first-known electric vehicle was a rail locomotive built by Aberdonian chemist, dyer and perfume-maker Robert Davidson in 1837.

6. A puckle souter an' tailor bodies, an' sic like trash

The tide of revolution that swept across America and France in the years of the late eighteenth and early nineteenth centuries lapped at the shores of Britain, raising hopes that the British government, built on class and privilege, might be reformed. When in 1832 parliament rejected two reform bills anger up and down the country was tangible.

Corruption was as rife at burgh and county levels as it was in national government and those campaigning to democratise it were condemned as dangerous radicals threatening national security. In Aberdeen a 'small coterie' of unelected and unaccountable magistrates were criticised in the press for running the city in their own interests. A single MP, elected by just five men, represented the royal burghs of Aberdeen, Inverbervie, Brechin, Arbroath and Montrose combined, while in the county 200 electors were instructed who to vote for by the Duke of Gordon.

Growing frustration with parliament's reluctance to reform itself stoked fury across the country with threats to withhold taxes and even take up arms to compel the king and

Little-known lithograph of a demonstration on the Broadhill in 1832 (courtesy of Aberdeen City Libraries).

his government to listen to popular opinion. During the days of May of 1832 when riots and demonstrations reached their zenith, government and monarchy feared the country was headed for revolution.

On Friday 18 May the Union flag was raised on the summit of the Broadhill. At the harbour colourful streamers and flags fluttered from ships' masts as a declaration of support for the Great Reform Act. Musicians congregated at neuks and closes as men and women arrived on foot, by horse and cart from Kintore, Inverurie and Monymusk. Bands struck up and people fell into line: blacksmiths, flax dressers, thread lappers, sawyers, weavers, bleachers, engineers, founders, and paper makers. They had banners flying, saying: 'Scotland and Liberty'; 'Deceived, but not defeated'; 'Let Kings beware'; 'Put not your trust in Princes'; 'Liberty or Death' and 'Reform or no Taxes' below a skull and crossbones; and a flag painted with three coffins and the maxim 'Taxes, Wellington, Bishops'.

To the strains of 'Scots wha hae wi Wallace bled and Blue bonnets o'er the Border' 40,000 snaked along Union Street. At Tory offices on Castle Street the crowd's frustration and anger exploded into a barrage of hisses and groans at PM Wellington and his party's opposition to reform.

Rich and poor united in their aspiration for change – hundreds then thousands and still they came: rope makers, tanners, tobacco spinners, carriers, ship wrights, white fishers, a hundred carters mounted on horses all keeping step to the beat set by the musicians. Forty thousand headed for the Links, appropriately by way of Constitution Street, to hear speeches on freedom and justice.

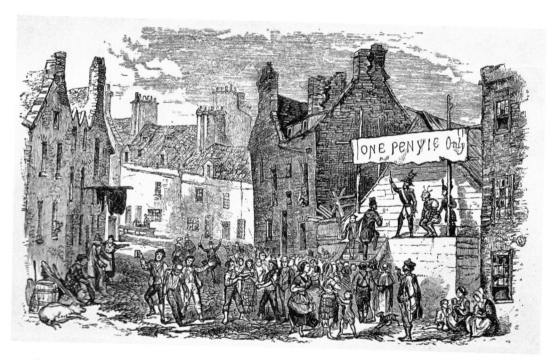

Penny Rattler street theatre on Albion Street (Bool Road), famous for agitation, infamous for drunkenness, prostitution and thieving.

Those crusaders for democracy did not have long to wait for their hopes to be dashed. The Great Reform Act was significant only as a precedent for future constitutional changes grudgingly granted over the next century by the peoples' 'enemies and deceivers'.

1832 introduced minor changes: 2,000 men were enfranchised in Aberdeen which at last got its own MP; royal burghs such as Aberdeen would in future be run by elected not appointed politicians to the fury of John Home, Town Keeper and dyed-in-the-wool Tory, who condemned burgh reforms for driving gentlemen such as Hadden and Cruden out of the council and replacing them with 'a puckle souter an' tailor bodies, an' sic like trash.'

Others at the Town House disagreed; one clerk took to verse to express his relief at the end of cronyism:

> In the year eighteen hundred and thirty-three,
> A very great change in this house is to be;
> The clerks, town-serjeants, town's drummers, and all,
> Must speedily, out of its door, 'tak' their crawl.'

Chartism

The 1832 reforms mainly improved representation for middle-class men and with that solidarity across the classes was ended. Having won some rights the middle classes largely turned their backs on the labouring classes to deny them the same. Not all, however, for the Chartists drew some support from across society with their call for universal suffrage, liberty and taxation with representation expressed in their charter as one man one vote at secret ballots, annual parliaments, paid MPs and removal of the property qualification to enable working men to enter parliament. Women were also active and initially were included in the Chartists' programme until it was argued men alone stood a greater chance of success.

'Sisters of bondage' was how Mrs Ogilvie of Aberdeen Female Radical Association described her fellow women struggling for liberty:

All capital springs from labour, and therefore the working classes having no capital are robbed of their hard-won earnings, and then taunted for being poor and ignorant.

(1839)

Maria Black was a factory hand and active Chartist. Chartism had two wings: physical or militant and moral or persuasive which led to strong feelings on both sides. When Fergus O'Connor, the physical wing's national leader rose to address a meeting in Aberdeen's Union Hall, dressed not in the Chartist colours of green and purple but a blue coat with gilt buttons over a yellow waistcoat, it was to a rendering of 'See the Conquering Hero Come' from a group playing fifes and heckling from a fellow-Irishman brandishing a large shillelagh. Maria presented O'Connor with a tartan plaid on behalf of mill women and was sacked from her job for so doing though reinstated following protests.

The wife of John Legge, stonemason, bookseller and first chairman of the Aberdeen Charter Union, was herself active and led a group of female Chartists in the city. Her husband condemned the government's 'class legislation' for creating the miserable conditions endured by working people arguing anything less than full suffrage would be a 'mockery of people's miseries'. Fellow Chartist, combmaker, James McPherson condemned those who:

> had made a profession of the destruction of men – that they made it their business to destroy their fellow creatures, and devoted their lives to carrying suffering to mankind.

When he stood for parliament in 1847 he urged electors:

> to rally round him and do away with class legislation and support reform for agitation might teach the people what they could accomplish

but most of those who had the vote would not support a Chartist.

The Chartist movement was very active, well organised and conspicuous on Aberdeen's streets. Maria Black's father John must have cut an imposing figure astride his white

Tucked into a hidden corner of St Peter's graveyard stands this symbolic and beautiful memorial to William Rennie, stonemason and socialist who died aged twenty-eight in 1894.

charger at the head of one of their demonstrations but when the horse's owner, a farmer from the Bridge of Don, discovered where his mount had been he complained that Black had turned the animal into a Chartist that, 'winna be o' muckle eese noo.'

Chartist newspapers kept supporters informed about activities nationwide but were priced beyond the pocket of most poor people so John Black set up a little enterprise whereby he bought a daily 4d newspaper and rented it out at a halfpenny for two hours. One of the city's several pro-Chartist tailors, Tawse from the Gallowgate, kept a collection of Chartist literature including its newspaper, the *Northern Star*, for anyone who wished to read them and his neighbour the bookseller William Lindsay stocked a range of Chartist publications, including their journals. Aberdeen's newspaper the *Herald* was fairly sympathetic to Chartism but the conservative *Aberdeen Journal* was hostile. Local pro-Chartist publications included the *Aberdeen Review, Aberdeen Patriot* and the *Northern Vindicator*, similar to the *Scottish Vindicator*, with its demand to set 'Scotland free', drawing inspiration from William Wallace.

Local publication, the *Shaver*, mocked radicalism and Chartism, describing those gathered in Aberdeen on New Year's day 1839 as a mob; 'tag-rag and bob-tail' and 'swinish multitude' talking humbug about securing the right to vote for folk who would go straight from agitating to the tippling shops and tap rooms to indulge in 'bumpers o pot-porter and raw-grain'. In fact Scottish Chartism was noted for its strong religious strain and closely linked with the temperance movement – John Legge for one – and would meet at the Temperance Hall on Queen Street if not the Union Hall in Blackfriars Street or Mother M'Onag's hotel in Exchequer Row.

Scottish Chartism was said to be diffident, content to rely on persuasion through rallies and petitions such as the 15,000 signatures collected around Aberdeen in condemnation of the death sentences imposed on Chartists at the 1839 Newport Rising in Wales. Perhaps one difficulty was the Chartist movement was organised centrally from England with many Scottish members unable to afford time off work and the cost of travelling hundreds of miles to meetings so decisions were taken without consultation with Scottish members. On occasions delegates travelling to meetings were far from diffident with one Aberdonian reporting to a national gathering that his city was armed and ready to rise.

Queen Street publisher, radical and poet John Mitchell of the Aberdeen Working Men's Association warned that the British state would not hesitate to use force to defend itself from the common man and cautioned his fellow Chartists to secrete weapons and be prepared to use them to defend 'your Queen, your country, and your liberty'. He condemned the tyrants in government and urged people to continue the struggle to achieve their birth right:

> Slaves will ye longer be? swear that ye shall be free!
> Tyranny's fetters each manly heart spurns;
> Stand where a Wallace stood, and where a Bruce hath trod -
> Hurra for the slave-hating spirit of Burns!
>
> Hurra for the Charter! hurra for the brave!

The 1840s brought hard times and unemployment to Aberdeen; one firm alone, Leys, Masson and Co. (Gordon Mills) paid off around one thousand hands when it shut down. International tensions with China and the ongoing revolutionary situation in France both unnerved and invigorated participants in the debate over democracy. Provost Blaikie condemned Aberdonians for being 'led astray by evil counsel' when they marched in the city against Britain's involvement in war on 8 October 1840 in the company of Chartist organiser Julian Harney.

In 1843 Aberdeen's bakers dressed in bright pink muslin and wearing exotic turbans led a colourful pageant of united trades with broadsword-wielding marshals clad in velvet riding extravagantly decorated horses. Such activity was good for morale but did not budge the government's resolve to thwart further extension of the franchise.

Aberdeen Chartists' congratulatory message to the French people for successfully quashing the ambitions of their king, Louis Phillipe, must have been written with a mixture of joy and envy.

The Links were again the venue for the largest demonstration for reform the city had seen since 1832 when on Saturday 16 August 1884 a rally was held in support of the partial enfranchisement of working class men. Three cheers were raised for Gladstone and three groans for the House of Lords, always opposed to extending the franchise, with the crowd making clear they were not for reforming the Lords but for ending it and its hereditary privileges.

Some of the 10,000 who marched in support of the Franchise Bill on 16 August 1884, at Guild Street (courtesy of Aberdeen City Libraries).

On another occasion reform demonstrators waved a large banner depicting a Conservative-supporting working man with the head of an ass. At that same rally a donkey was criticised for its Conservative sympathies when it refused to carry a stuffed effigy of Tory PM Lord Salisbury on its back. Fortunately Kirkie's sand cart came to the rescue and 'the man of straw' was taken away to his meet his fate on top of a bonfire.

Among the many trades represented on that day were eighty men from Gordon Mills in carpet aprons and sporting rosettes; employees of Broadford's, Bannermill and Ben Reid's; quarriers from Rubislaw marching shoulder to shoulder with farm labourers from Kemnay and Peterculter, Monymusk and Tillyfour. Always prominent, the city's bakers this time in white aprons and caps with rolled-up shirt sleeves, held up three types of loaves to the amusement of onlookers: the Gladstone loaf, the Franchise loaf and what the Tories would give you loaf.

The reluctance of parliament to create anything like a just system truly representative of the country only served to make each generation more determined to succeed. Women had to battle not only the entrenched resistance of Westminster but reactionary attitudes generally. It is regrettable so many men, including trades unionists who were also victims of injustice, opposed women in their struggle for equality.

Suffragettes

Women had battled alongside men throughout the nineteenth century for a British parliament worthy of its name. They had been abandoned after 1832 in the vain hope that working men might be quickly emancipated but continued their own struggle while enduring ridicule from all sides.

Women, with the exception of the Queen, were judged inferior to men. Working women were regarded as the most worthless of all, even by some Suffragettes. It was not from the hazardous, noisy mills that the suffragists and suffragettes emerged but mainly from middle and upper-class homes – educated and privileged women who had the confidence to voice their opinions. Counted among aristocratic supporters of women's suffrage was the Countess of Aberdeen, chairman of the Women's Liberal Federation (WLF). She had no time for militancy and wrote to Campbell-Bannerman PM in 1906 disassociating the WLF from all direct action. The Dugdale sisters from Aboyne, too, were well-heeled supporters of the cause. Una Dugdale, an organiser in Aberdeen, caused a national sensation by omitting 'obey' from her wedding vows when marrying Victor Duval of the Men's Political Union for Women's Enfranchisement.

For all their advantages prosperous women were valued mainly as ornament or source of wealth while working-class women were a labour resource and readily exploitable. A correspondent to *Aberdeen Journal* wrote of a woman clerk she knew being paid one-third the amount a man earned for the same work and of a young woman, the breadwinner for herself and widowed mother, having her pay reduced from 8 to 3s because her employer, a prominent Aberdonian, knew her desperation would make her accept any wage.

Aberdeen Suffrage Society (ASS) was set-up in 1871 with a Mrs Bain of Ferryhill Lodge its secretary. Her colleague Miss McCombie was possibly the daughter of William McCombie, editor of the city's progressive newspaper *Aberdeen Free Press* and cousin of the breeder of Aberdeen Angus cattle. As with Chartism the women suffrage movement

Suffragette Helen Fraser campaigning in the 1908 Kincardineshire by-election (courtesy of Aberdeenshire Libraries).

included militant and non-militant factions. The National Union of Women's Suffrage Society (NUWSS) known as Suffragists spent decades arguing their case while the Women's Social and Political Union (WSPU) dubbed Suffragettes chose direct action out of exasperation hence their motto 'deeds not words'. In 1905 the ASS affiliated with the NUWSS but it was the militant WSPU which attracted all the headlines.

Aberdeen and Aberdeenshire had become centres of Liberalism and so the Suffragette movement took their fight with the Liberal government to the Northeast with Adela Pankhurst and Helen Fraser dispatched north to organise. In fact every major name associated with the movement found her way to Aberdeen with a number detained in Craiginches prison and a few manhandled by members of Shore Porters, apparently used as heavies. There were successes too as when the WSPU succeeded in slashing a Liberal majority from 4,000 to under 400 at a by-election in Aberdeen South in 1907. In these altered times it seems hardly credible to read of their acts of arson, smashing windows, destroying mail, chaining themselves outside public buildings and of course the famous incident when Emily Davison dog-whipped a church minister she mistook for Lloyd George at the Joint Station.

Much of the protest was good-natured. When Liberal candidate for Kincardineshire Captain Arthur Murray took to the stump in April 1908 he was surprised to find three suffragettes already addressing his audience of 100 men at Harpers yard at Craiginches. With some difficulty he gained their attention but the WSPU's Mary Gawthorpe stole them back with her witty rhetoric and 'fog and frost' voice. The neglected Murray was forced into retreat to cries of 'Keep out the Liberal' and 'hear, hear' ringing in his ears.

DISGUISED!

Left: Anti-Suffragette cartoon lampooning them and the Liberal government in *Bon-Accord,* 1906.

Below: WSPU headquarters were at the Crown Mansions, No. 41 1/2 Union Street.

Mary Gawthorpe was no friend of the Liberal Party. At a public meeting in Banchory in 1908 she subdued one heckler with, 'I must remind you this is not a Liberal meeting – questions afterwards, and you will not be thrown out' (a reference to the ejection of an elderly minister for daring to ask a question on women's suffrage at a Liberal Party meeting in the Music Hall). Miss Gawthorpe subdued another man in the audience with the retort, 'You should have been born a woman, you cannot stop talking'.

In November that year Prime Minister Asquith's candidature for the rectorship of Aberdeen University united the forces of the WSPU and NUWSS and created tensions within the Women's Liberal Association forcing members to choose between the party and the cause. There was friction, too, between Aberdeen's secretary of the WSPU Caroline Phillips, *Aberdeen Daily Journal*'s first woman reporter, and the Pankhursts over tactics. Relations became glacial when in 1909 in a display of contemptuous arrogance London organisers decided unilaterally to centralise the movement in London under the banner of the National WSPU, instructing local groups, including Aberdeen, to be dissolved. At this point Caroline Phillips was removed from her role in Aberdeen by the Pankhursts who thereafter kept a tight rein on activities in city.

By alienating Caroline Phillips the movement lost a bonnie fechter who chained herself to railings, destroyed mail in pillar-boxes, practised the art of 'silent shop-window-breaking at night' in the best WSPU tradition and was in the raiding party that sneaked into Balmoral's grounds swapping its putting green flags for ones declaring Votes for Women.

Irrespective of factional feuds support for women's emancipation remained strong in the city as demonstrated when hundreds gathered to listen to Sylvia Pankhurst speak at the Wallace statue early in 1909 although she was attacked by a group of stone-throwing boys.

The local press became another battleground for expressing opinions. It has to be said the most abusive letters were from those opposed to women's emancipation often reducing the suffrage movement to nothing more than an exhibition by 'mannish women'.

Pro-suffrage arguments tended to be along the lines that women paid taxes and rates yet were denied representation. They disposed of the smear that women lacked the intelligence to vote declaring stupidity never precluded any man from voting.

An opposing view was that women were inferior to men in every way: less intelligent, less capable and should be grateful for having men take decisions for them. Some argued against educating women as it would be detrimental to families; that women should obey their husbands and fathers; that pro-suffrage women were Amazonians who screeched and made themselves into a laughing-stock; that such women should instead earn the respect of men by spending their time teaching the poor better habits.

Leonora Lockhart of Bridge of Don and Mrs Lockhart from Donbank both staunch anti-reformers expressed their fears for 'the race' and British Empire at a meeting in the Music Hall in November 1911. They warned that if women were granted a vote working-class mothers would neglect their boys who would grow up into weak men. Mrs Lockhart declared women were superior to men in some ways but, 'man had the advantage in the last resort because his elemental supremacy must prevail' and if women were ever admitted to parliament they could face a revolt over their 'women-made laws'

AT-THE SUFFRAGETTE MEETING

Suffragettes attracted a share of 'the bucolic wit of the auction marts' in 1908 (courtesy of Aberdeenshire Libraries).

and without the protection of men woman-kind would face their Armageddon and be thrown into 'oppression and slavery' by resentful men.

Their fatuous views were challenged in a letter to the *Aberdeen Journal*:

Do the Mrs Lockharts ever hear the Broadford bell ringing at half-past five in the morning? and does it ever occur to them that while they are lying comfortably in bed for another three or four hours on these cold, wet, dismal days, hundreds of poor women are rushing to earn the pittance that keeps body and soul together? ... Where is the men's obligation of considering, working for, and protecting these poor women?

Women were increasingly drawn into politics albeit locally through district and parish councils, school boards and so on and while various Women's Conciliation Bills, designed to extend the franchise to wealthy property-owning women, had been introduced into parliament between 1910 and 1912 with all voted down.

The work undertaken by some women during the First World War is often cited as earning them the right to the vote but no government could risk a return to pre-war militancy by denying women's suffrage. The Representation of the People Act 1918 gave all adult males and the majority of women over thirty years old the vote but it was not until 1928 that women achieved equal suffrage with men.

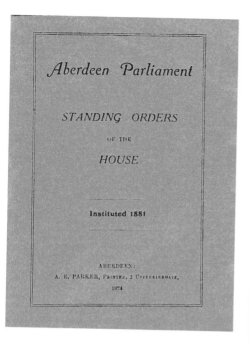

Above: Aberdeen Parliament rule book.

Right: Aberdeen Parliament Coalition Cabinet, 1927–28.

THE ABERDEEN PARLIAMENT.

SIXTY-SECOND SESSION, 1927-28.

COALITION MINISTRY.

Prime Minister and First Lord of the Treasury	Mr. JAMES LONGMORE.
Chancellor of the Exchequer	Mr. J. M'HATTIE.
Secretary of State for Foreign Affairs	Mr. R. JOHNSTON.
Secretary of State for Home Affairs	Mr. H. DOW.
Secretary of State for Colonial Affairs	Mr. G. COWIE, Jun.
Secretary of State for Indian Affairs	Mr. R. W. ORMISTON.
Secretary of State for Scotland	Mr. W. J. M'KAY.
Minister of Defence	Maj. R. SHAW MACPHAIL.
Lord Advocate	Mr. A. T. T. WHITEHOUSE.
Minister of Agriculture	Mr. T. CORALL.
Minister of Health	Mr. J. MURISON.
Minister of Labour and Mines	Mr. W. YOUNG.
Minister of Pensions	Mr. J. C. MITCHELL.
President, Board of Trade	Mr. W. KILLIN.
President, Board of Education	Mr. A. J. ANDERSON.
Postmaster-General	Mr. J. C. FOTHERINGHAM.
Commissioner of Works	Mr. T. LEIPER.

Did You Know?

A popular debating society called the Aberdeen Parliament, which ran from the mid-1880s to the mid-1930s, was organised along the lines of the House of Commons with its own Prime Minister, ministers and speaker, cabinet, opposition, debates and votes.

7. Shawlie Wifies and Barefoot Bairns

Advances in the care of Britain's women and children during the twentieth century owe a debt of gratitude to two Aberdeen doctors – Dugald Baird and Mary Esslemont. They were almost exact contemporaries but from different social backgrounds; Esslemont's was one of privilege – her family prominent Aberdeen Liberals who put the Esslemont into Esslemont and Macintosh department store – while Baird was the son of a science teacher from Ayrshire. Baird's name and reputation would become as synonymous with the city as native Aberdonian Mary Esslemont.

From the 1930s to the 1970s Baird and Esslemont were significant among a body of distinguished doctors who made Aberdeen into a leader in social medicine. Both took first degrees in science before entering medicine and for all her privileges Mary Esslemont battled against convention and out-and-out male chauvinism for most of her life, succeeding against the odds to achieve prominence as a leading specialist in women's and children's care. Among her influences was her mother, Clementina, who as a young woman was prevented because of her gender from graduating in medicine and only received her degree in 1941, and Aberdeen's first woman General Practitioner, Elizabeth Latto Ewan. Ewan who was the youngest recipient of the Scottish triple qualification in 1895 went on to specialise in midwifery and women's diseases. Esslemont, known as Dr Mary, had a practice which took in the working-class district of Torry from where she pursued her interest in the health of women and children in particular and from where she and her mother offered care to the children of travelling people who over-wintered in the city.

Newly qualified doctor Dugald Baird was horrified by the extent of poverty he encountered in Glasgow and despaired at how multiple pregnancies ravaged the health of its working-class women. He criticised the indifferent service provided for the poor such as insufficient blood supplies that might save the lives of women haemorrhaging during childbirth and was disciplined and branded disloyal for speaking out on the matter. Baird wanted to shake up the medical establishment in Glasgow to improve care for its most needy but he was met with huge resistance which he attributed to the overbearing influence of religion on all aspects of life in that city, including medicine, and which he judged responsible for condemning women and babies to a lifetime of poor health.

The frustrations Baird experienced in Glasgow encouraged him to take up the post of Regius Professor of Midwifery at the University of Aberdeen in 1937. In Aberdeen he found the city both progressive and liberal minded, not held back by the weight of religious dogma. In addition Aberdeen's size made it ideal to study the impact of socio-economic factors on infant well-being. Aberdeen already had a centralised medical service which enabled Baird to coordinate his findings on the suspected link between the environment and good or poor health.

Above left: Dr Esslemont BSc (1914), MA (1915), MBChB (1923) – all at Aberdeen (MS3179/5/2/3/ graduation Aberdeen University, Special Collections Centre).

Above right: Alberto Morrocco's portrait of Professor Dugald Baird (courtesy of Aberdeen Medico-Chirurgical Society).

Baird would become one of the most far-sighted and important obstetricians in Britain and his Maternity & Neonatal Data Bank, with its meticulous and unique record-keeping on patients, an important reservoir of research material for medical science far beyond Aberdeen.

Improvements in women's and infant health that occurred in the era of Esslemont and Baird were continuums of medical innovation in the city over centuries.

The first medical school in Britain was established in Aberdeen, founded by Bishop Elphinstone in 1495 at King's College (the town's first recorded medical practitioner was Donald Bannerman in the fourteenth century). The first Regius Professor of Medicine in British Isles, James Cumyne, was appointed at King's in Old Aberdeen by James IV in 1497, nearly half a century before the often-quoted one at Oxford. King's offered the first degrees in medicine in Scotland and taught aspects of medicine under the more general scholarship of a mediciner – the first appointee some say was Cumyne in 1505, others claim Gilbert Skene in 1568. Skene's course taught entirely in Latin, encompassed theology, law and the arts as well as medicine and was unique in the British Isles and similar to that offered at the universities of Paris and Bologna. King's graduates often continued their medical education at other European universities where several also

This illustration *c.* 1670 depicts Aberdeen's first university King's College which was founded in 1495.

taught, including Leyden, Helmstedt and St Petersburg. In another first for the city doctorates in medicine were awarded, ahead of other Scottish universities by nearly forty years in 1630, the first recipient was a Mr Parkin.

Not all was admirable, despite the city's pioneering reputation in medical studies, and in an attempt to improve their medical education a group of students in 1789 formed a society to provide extra-mural lectures at the city's second university, Marischal College. Formed as the Medical Society, Aberdeen it became the Medico-Chirurgical Society with its own building in King Street, complete with a fine library and museum. The society's founder James McGrigor went on to become the 'Father of the Army Medical Service' and was responsible for army medical care in Spain and France during the Napoleonic Wars. An obelisk honouring him was erected at Marischal but now stands in Duthie Park.

For 500 years Aberdeen has been central to scholarship in medicine, including obstetrics. In the eighteenth century midwifery classes were offered, indeed the city got its first male midwife then, David Skene (who studied midwifery at university in Paris). When obstetric forceps, invented a century earlier, were more widely adopted in the eighteenth century childbirth moved within the realm of obstetricians rather than midwives.

Births normally took place in the home but in 1742 Aberdeen opened its first lying-in facility for the poor and home visits were provided along with the first of several dispensaries offering medicines and advice (later brought together as the Aberdeen General Dispensary, Vaccine and Lying-in Institution) supplying medicine free, *medicine gratis.*

Former Aberdeen Medico-Chirurgical building on King Street with its impressive portico. The society is now based at the Medical School, Foresterhill.

William Adam's Marischal College before Archibald Simpson's renovations of the 1840s.

Care of pregnant women, among the poor in particular, was offered by the infirmary from 1762 with its midwife Mrs Jean Baird paying one guinea per year. Aberdeen doctor Alexander Gordon was instrumental, well before Semmelweis, in identifying the causes of childbed fever or puerperal sepsis, hugely infectious and a great cause of death in young women from poor hygiene. In the city mothers from the worst slums were provided with a safe and hygienic place to deliver their babies, initially at a small house in Barnett's Close.

When Aberdeen's two universities, King's and Marischal, combined in 1860 real progress in relation to medicine followed, including the establishment of Britain's first Professorship of Midwifery. By the 1890s six qualified midwives were employed by the Dispensary. Castlehill was chosen for the first children's hospital because of its open sunny and breezy aspect and proximity to the city's poorer districts of the east end. From small beginnings of fourteen beds in 1877 it quickly grew to accommodate sixty patients.

In 1906 when it was made statutory to provide pregnant women and young children with medical care Aberdeen could look back on half a century of such provision. Within six years the city's first proper maternity hospital opened at Castle Terrace, later transferring to Foresterhill in 1937 at a cost of £52,000, borne entirely by public subscription – so much for the myth of the mean Aberdonian. Here at last was a first class provision, entirely free, unusual before the National Health Service, run by a voluntary board and supported by the local council. From 1919 the city had its own child welfare clinics in

Castlehill Barracks dominates this drawing of *c.* 1850 but to the left is hangman's brae, later Castle Terrace and site of the first Sick Children's Hospital in 1877.

addition to voluntary and charitable centres and pre-natal and ante-natal services as part of its maternity and child welfare provision.

By now hospital births were becoming more common, driven by the medical profession's attempts to reduce infant deaths. In 1950 Aberdeen boasted the lowest infant mortality rate ever recorded in Scotland – testament to the excellence of its care of pregnant and nursing mothers and their babies.

	0–1 month	1–12 month(s)	Total
1904–08	41	93	134
1938	33	38	71
1950	16	12	28

Infant Mortality in Aberdeen per thousand live births

Aberdeen recognised the importance of maternal well-being for both mother and child for lowering deaths during pregnancy and childbirth and it was the safest place in Scotland to have a baby between 1933 and 1946. The poor were especially vulnerable to maternal and infant mortality and Baird and Esslemont were determined to tackle this iniquity.

Esslemont was active in groups such as International Planned Parenthood while Baird, in his role as Professor of Midwifery, stressed the necessity of conferring choice to women – their 5th Freedom as he termed it – freedom from the tyranny of excessive fertility, a reference to US President Franklin Roosevelt's Four Freedoms: of speech; worship; from want; from fear. Baird had in mind the average fifteen years of pregnancy experienced by working-class women reduced to just four by the 1950s thanks in part to practices carried out in Aberdeen.

Attitudes relating to social medicine were changing by the early twentieth century including issues surrounding birth control and family planning. With births exceeding deaths by 300,000 annually the Royal College of General Practitioners worried about over-population. By contrast Baird and Esslemont were keen to relieve women of the burden of multiple pregnancies which depleted their health and turned them old beyond their years and to improve the health of expectant mothers so their babies had a greater chance of survival. Certainly the question of birth control divided opinion. For some it was a passing phase, a symptom of immorality, an unhealthy passion for freedom, atheistic and harbinger of diseases including cancer. Without birth control others warned of impending famine, epidemics and threats to world peace. Most controversial of all were the eugenicists who favoured reproduction through selection. The eminent biologist Professor Julian Huxley condemned large working-class families as a threat likely to overwhelm the wealthy classes – a state-of-affairs that did not occur a century earlier, he claimed, and the consequence of the middle classes practising methods of birth control while denying the same to the poor with welfare clinics prohibited from giving advice on family planning.

At the height of this controversy in the mid-1920s the Birth Control Committee of the Aberdeen Mother and Child Welfare Association, founded by Clementine Esslemont, opened Scotland's first birth control clinic at No. 4 Gerrard Street in the Gallowgate. Open Monday to Friday from 10.00 a.m. to 6.00 p.m. the clinic consciously reached out

A house in the Guestrow or Ghaistrow near St Nicholas' graveyard. Poor housing, unsanitary conditions and overcrowding led to sickness and premature death (courtesy of Aberdeen City Libraries).

to working-class women. Dr Fenella Paton who ran the clinic was a disciple of Dr Marie Stopes with whom she had worked in London. Gerrard Street's Constructive Birth Clinic was innovative and a vital source of guidance for those worn down by the drudgery of unplanned pregnancies which condemned families to ever-deepening poverty.

Gerrard Street attracted inevitable criticism and was condemned as an 'affront to Aberdeen's civic morality' by Dr James Hay. His opinion was supported by Professor McKerron, then Chair of Midwifery at the University of Aberdeen, who was vehemently opposed to working-class women knowing about birth control. In his view large families were usually the healthiest and happiest, 'the more the merrier,' able to 'lick each other into shape' and with sensible budgeting even the poorest could get along. McKerron dismissed the clinic's doctor as a 'junior lady practitioner' lacking the 'necessary knowledge or experience to give advice on this important and highly controversial subject' and accused her of placing medicine in Aberdeen in a bad light. He was fearful for the survival of the white 'race' if birth control reduced the number of white children, those in the 'highest order of race', while doing nothing to stem growing populations of black and yellow inferior 'races'.

Undaunted by such extremist views the clinic's staff: Dr Flossie Malcolm, Dr Paton, nurse Mrs Rae and soon Dr Mary Esslemont persevered on their shoe-string budget and open-door policy to inform and provide contraception to any married women who sought their help.

The clinic briefly came under the Marie Stopes organisation but as the Aberdeen Gynaecological Advisory Clinic continued until 1948 when it was brought under the auspices of the Public Health Committee of Aberdeen Corporation making the city the first local authority in the country to run such a facility and maintaining Aberdeen's prominence in family planning.

The formation of the National Health Service in 1948 was a landmark in healthcare in the UK when the sick no longer had to scrape together sufficient funds to pay for essential medicines and care or be dependent on charity such as provided by Aberdeen Dispensary at Castle Terrace which in the October of 1935 during Esslemont's time in charge of its gynaecological department issued over 5000 free prescriptions to the city's most needy.

Mary Esslemont and Dugald Baird first met at a meeting on birth control when she spoke of the pioneering work being done in Aberdeen. Baird, who would go on to write

Right: Gerrard Street off the Gallowgate where Aberdeen's first family planning clinic was opened.

Below: Local medical students temporarily lived in while training in obstetrics and midwifery at Aberdeen Dispensary and Lying-in Institution during the 1930s when Dr Esslemont was in charge of its gynaecological department.

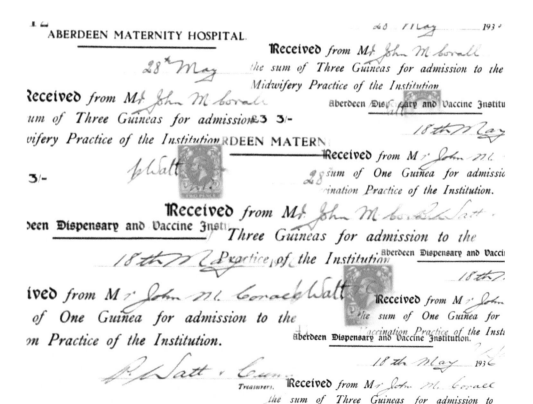

the first textbook on contraception, was familiar with Marie Stope's work on planned parenthood and her views largely chimed in with his own having witnessed many needless deaths of young women through complications of pregnancy, multiple pregnancies and illegal abortions. In 1936 Baird expressed the opinion 'it was the good mother and not the bad one who dreaded the coming of many children.' He was committed to provide women with a degree of control over their lives along with a first-class service of care for them and their infants. In pursuit of this he recruited a team of equally brilliant and enthusiastic doctors and scientists known as 'Baird's boys'.

Dugald Baird had scarcely settled into Aberdeen before expanding the scope of its birth control provision. In addition to providing advice and contraceptives women with seven or more children were offered abortions and sterilisation. It is said this was the first time abortions were officially carried out in the city, a practice he never would have been able to offer in Glasgow where Baird found doctors took a high-handed attitude towards what they regarded was in their patients' best interests, usually based on the doctors' own religious prejudices; in Baird's opinion a doctor's role should be only advisory. He consulted with his patients, listening to women describe their particular circumstances while seeking their views on whether to continue or terminate pregnancies, and encouraged his students to do likewise. A story is told of one former patient who years later recognised the eminent doctor in a bus queue. She spoke to him insisted on paying

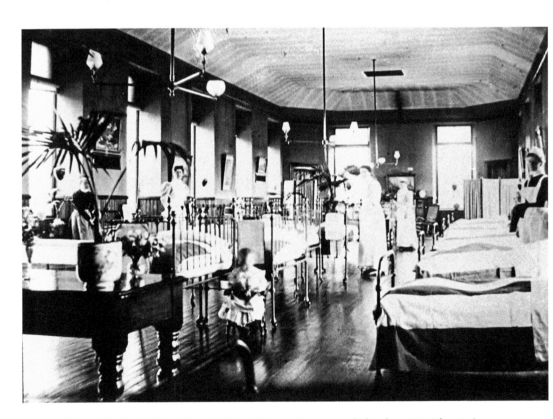

Gas-lit ward in the children's hospital Castle Terrace (courtesy of Aberdeen City Libraries).

his fare and they sat together on the bus. Few of his contemporaries would have been so at ease, nor former patients so relaxed in the company of their obstetrician.

Esslemont's commitment to women and children's health was as determined as Baird's and she enjoyed a warm reputation among the women and children under her care. A lifelong member of the British Medical Association she was the only Scot and only woman involved in discussions with Aneurin Bevan and the government in the mid-1940s prior to the establishment of the NHS which she urged should promote preventative medicine or 'positive health' of the kind already being pursued in Aberdeen.

It is hard to overstate Aberdeen health authority's impressive record and radical approach to medicine and provision for women and children before the NHS.

When in 1966 an Abortion Bill was being drawn up in parliament it was Baird's pioneering work in Aberdeen that proved crucial to the final wording of the Act, including his suggestion of a single socio-medical clause for deciding on terminations. Interestingly Scots law allowed for terminations to be carried out if regarded as being in the best interests of the mother but it seems only in Aberdeen this was practised to any extent. Baird's courageous insistence that social as well as medical grounds should be considered in determining abortion made him the target of much criticism. He was surely iron-willed for the medical fraternity was by nature deeply conservative, not to say reactionary, and Baird's work challenged its deep-set prejudices. He and Esslemont, along with many of their colleagues, forced the medical establishment to reconsider how women and their fertility were regarded.

The excellence of medical provision in Aberdeen was the result of cooperation between the university, hospitals, GPs and Aberdeen Corporation. Aberdeen Council took over the running of the city's family planning service in 1948 and by 1967 it had become entirely free and hugely progressive in outlook, providing first-class care to women, married and single. Life-saving cervical screening, now a universal service, was pioneered in Aberdeen with Dr Elizabeth Macgregor in charge, at the invitation of Dugald Baird in 1960.

What was different in Aberdeen was its holistic approach to women's and children's health – a comprehensive and freely accessible service offering choice to women (and their families) backed up by its impressive Maternity & Neonatal Databank.

The birth rate in Aberdeen dropped steadily and ahead of the rest of Scotland. With such high levels of care Aberdeen suffered no maternal deaths whatsoever in 1969 and 1970. Fewer women died in low-income Aberdeen than in the affluent south of England and its infant mortality rates in the early 1970s were among the lowest in the world. At a time when illegitimacy mattered the rate in Aberdeen fell by an astounding one-fifth in 1971–72 while numbers rose elsewhere in Scotland.

The introduction of the pill in 1964 revolutionised birth control with more resources going into family planning nationally. The pill which promised easy, reliable contraception claimed to be a safeguard against breast cancer and excessive ear wax! There were calls to sell it in supermarkets and while Baird did not go that far he advocated it be prescribed to single women.

Some remained steadfastly opposed to Aberdeen's progressive approach to family planning. Of husbands who objected to their wives seeking contraception Aberdeen's Medical Officer of Health, Dr Ian MacQueen, observed that it was no longer acceptable for a man to think he owned his wife and that women most in need of an IUD were married to men most hostile to contraception.

Mary Esslemont found women, especially working-class women, were increasingly willing to seek help with planning their families as a result of provisions within the NHS and the free and open services available in Aberdeen. The benefits were healthier mothers and babies.

The city's family planning service came at a price. In 1960 the cost was £3,000 but by 1967, when contraceptives were distributed free in the city, costs almost quadrupled to £11,000 and by 1972, when women and girls could self-refer themselves to the clinic, that figure swelled to a mighty £31,000. The increasing costs reflected the popularity of the service; from fewer than 500 individual attendees in 1960 to around 1,500 by 1970. City students constituted the largest group of single women presenting at the clinic followed by clerical, then manual and finally professional women, including nurses and teachers; it may have been this last group preferred to get their contraceptives and advice from their GPs. As a means of liberating women from the 'slavery' of their fertility the monetary cost was the price of success. In Aberdeen the birth rate dropped to the lowest of any Scottish city. Aberdeen's reputation was another matter for its progressive attitude to birth control earned it the name Sin City from a sensationalist press.

Undaunted the city's medical fraternity persevered with their advanced approach to reproductive health. As ignorance was a major reason for unplanned pregnancies so sex education was promoted in city schools in an attempt to encourage responsible behaviour

Aberdeen Family Planning Clinic was for a time in Bon Accord Square.

High-density housing in the centre of Aberdeen (courtesy of Aberdeen City Libraries).

among young people. Many will recall the ground-breaking series *Living and Growing* from the 1970s, produced by Aberdeen's Grampian Television.

Aberdeen's achievements emerged from a culture deeply rooted in the city's past and fostered by Baird and Esslemont and their contemporaries. Baird's world-class research team of dieticians, sociologists, physiologist, psychologist and epidemiologist provided the rigour to the social medicine experiment carried out in the city. His radical approach, remarkable Data Bank and good practice impressed and was supported by the Medical Research Council:

> the most impressive work in obstetrics I have met in this country, and that I have seen what appears to be a model of how the approach of social medicine can be effectively used in the strategy of research into a clinical problem (Sir Harold Himsworth – Medical Research Council).

Baird recognised the 'unrivalled opportunities' that enabled his successes were attributable to the liberal-minded city of Aberdeen, close links between the university and hospital and the remarkable Rowett Institute under John Boyd Orr whose ground-breaking work on nutrition led to the free distribution of orange juice, cod liver oil and milk to young children.

In Aberdeen patients were treated as individuals. The city was not afraid to be bold such as employing the first male health visitor. Its radical approach to family planning, first class ante-natal and post-natal services are testament to its forward-thinking. Births

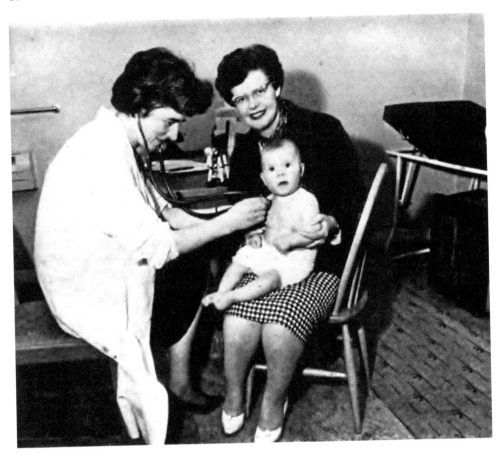

A child welfare clinic in Aberdeen.

were followed up in child welfare clinics and nurseries that offered advice on hygiene, budgeting, baby care, nutrition, social and personal problems, exercise, blood-tests, immunisations, dental care and so on because patients were people living rounded lives.

Problem pregnancies were dealt with at Foresterhill with the latest technology monitoring deliveries but most women did not require this level of provision and small maternity homes meant mothers could have their babies within their communities. Infant mortality plummeted in Aberdeen to twelve in every 1,000 live births in 1971 compared with the Scottish rate of twenty while in the mid-1960s Aberdeen's infant mortality at nineteen per 1,000 births was almost half that in Glasgow where thirty-six babies died in every 1,000.

The undimmed vision of both Professor Baird and Dr Esslemont set the standard for other areas to follow. Hugely energetic, Esslemont was an inveterate participant in international health conferences and the exchange of ideas. During a visit to the Soviet Union in 1936 she saw how infants were allocated a doctor for their first three years at a ratio of 500 children per doctor through child and parenthood clinics. That may have influenced the approach taken in Aberdeen when a series of children's welfare centres were planned on similar lines – the first opening in Torry in 1937 included a well-provisioned nursery where 'spontaneous development' was encouraged among its pre-school children. Sociability, friendliness and consideration were taught in the attractive and airy single-storey building with verandas, bathrooms, a laundry and kitchen. Spacious grounds and play areas included a large sand pit and jungle gymnasium. In an attempt to counter deprivation its initial intake were children from needy families or those suffering illness including psychological problems for the clinic offered time with doctors and health visitors. Similar nurseries and clinics popped up around the city – at the Castlegate, Charlotte Street, Holburn, Hilton and Northfield where children might be vaccinated against smallpox, diphtheria, whooping cough and the like and Charlotte Street, Hilton and Torry clinics where ultra-violet light sessions were provided for youngsters suffering from rickets and other bone diseases through a lack of vitamin D from too little exposure to natural sunlight.

For Aberdeen in the first half of the twentieth century to have had one such significant and dynamic doctor willing to shake-up the medical profession in the pursuit of improving care for all classes of women and children would have been admirable but for there to be a whole cluster of which I have chosen two, as well as the outstanding influence of Boyd Orr was remarkable. Doctor May Baird, Dugald Baird's wife, an influential figure in her own right and at the heart of free contraception within the city and active on the Health Committee and the Regional Hospital Board observed, 'It was simply a coming together of the right people at the right time'.

Children lacking vitamin D receiving ultra-violet treatment at Woodend Hospital in 1927 (courtesy of NHS Grampian Archives).

It is typical of Aberdeen that it wears its achievements lightly and does not feel the need to sing its own praises but perhaps it is just a little too diffident over its accomplishments. As for the rest of the world looking on not only was Aberdeen the Granite City then Sin City but also labelled the abortion capital of Britain as well. Another cost of progress.

The forward thinking of both Professor Baird and Dr Esslemont proved of enormous benefit to the people of Aberdeen. Their holistic approach to medicine combined with detailed scientific research embedded within a framework of social responsibility for the most vulnerable working-class mother and her infant led to exceptional levels of good practice and became an exemplar for the rest of the world. As part of its comprehensive approach to social responsibility the city authorities made improvements in housing and sanitation which had been as bad as in any other city and succeeded in improving standards of living and lowering infection rates.

There is little doubt that both Baird and Esslemont were motivated by down-to-earth humanity towards their fellow beings but they were not typical of the conservative

Sick children out in the fresh air on a balcony at the Sick Children's Hospital, Castle Terrace (courtesy of Aberdeen City Libraries).

medical establishment. Professor Baird had no misconceptions about how he was perceived by many of his contemporaries. A report in the *New Scientist* in 1974 quotes him saying he was regarded as a 'rather dangerous individual slashing away at the moral fibre of the nation' by his peers at the Royal College of Obstetricians and Gynaecologists. Despite his ground-breaking work Baird was never invited to deliver a major paper to that grand institution, a situation he found 'so ludicrous as to be amusing'. And of course he was never 'invited' to be president of the college.

Dr Esslemont's impact on the lives of Aberdonians has been immense and reflects her intellect and ambition: to become the first female president of the Students' Representative Council in Aberdeen in 1922 (and the last one for nearly seventy years); first female assessor on the university court; first woman to sit on the Scottish Council and its chairman; only female doctor included in a study visit comparing British with the Soviet health service in 1956; only female doctor on the body negotiating the NHS; the BMA representative at the World Medical Association; Honorary Life President of the United Nations Association in Scotland; active within the World Health Organisation, I could go on. Her contribution to the improvement of women's and children's health is unquestionable. She was as comfortable addressing her international audiences as she was delivering her series of lectures entitled 'Bringing up Baby' to parents in Aberdeen.

Dr Mary Esslemont on an official visit to the Soviet Union in 1956 (MS3179/5/2/3/plane Aberdeen University, Special Collections Centre).

Professor Dugald Baird's and Dr May Baird's house, Albyn Place.

In 1995 the University of Aberdeen opened the Dugald Baird Centre for Research on Women's Health, 'to improve the reproductive health of women and the health of their families' drawing on Baird's multi-disciplinary approach to research so continuing the advances begun by him, and indeed those with longer historic roots in the city.

Dr Esslemont, Professor Baird and his wife Dr May Baird were given the Freedom of the City of Aberdeen for their immense contributions to medicine. Esslemont was awarded a CBE in 1955 and Baird was knighted in 1959, six years before he retired.

Dr Mary Esslemont was the 'great trooper who lived her long life to the full' according to her obituary in the *British Medical Journal* following her death at the age of ninety-three in 1984. When Professor Dugald Baird died aged eighty-seven in 1986 the *British Medical Journal* described him as

> An outspoken leader and teacher of great character, he was also distinguished for his friendliness, compassion, and deep interest in people. The families of Aberdeen owe much to his understanding and resolution.

Modesty, humour, ambition and ability were the very traits that resulted in Dugald Baird and Mary Esslemont achieving so much – and not least their deep humanity. For their shared strength of purpose and undimmed vision for helping others we should be grateful.

Did You Know?

Between 1596 and 1826 Aberdeen had as many universities as all of England – two. Dr Agnes Thomson, active during the first half of the twentieth century, was a founding member of the Medical Women's Federation, influential in women's and baby health and instrumental in establishing Aberdeen's Mother and Baby Home.

Dr Arnold Klopper who was forced out of his native South Africa because of his opposition to apartheid became a Baird's Boy and one of the foremost endocrinologists of his age. His research into oestrogens in human pregnancy brought him worldwide recognition and a prize in his name is awarded annually by Aberdeen University to the student showing greatest distinction in obstetrics and gynaecology. Aberdeen was the first city to offer men vasectomies as part of family planning.

8. Milk and Oranges

Money can't buy good health, or can it? Certainly a lack of money can seriously damage one's health. So concluded a study carried out in Aberdeen in the 1920s when the city was establishing its credentials as an important centre of nutritional science.

The fertile farmlands of Northeast Scotland were the ideal locality for a North of Scotland College of Agriculture which was opened at Bucksburn in 1904. A Chair of Agriculture at the University of Aberdeen followed and in association with these two bodies a third emerged to develop the science of animal nutrition, the Rowett Institute, named after the businessman philanthropist Dr John Quiller Rowett whose funding was crucial to its establishment.

From its inception in 1910 it would take another twelve years to the Rowett's opening mainly due to the interruption of the First World War. So it was in 1922 that

John Orr with Queen Mary at the official opening of the Rowett in 1922 (MSU1451/RRI/1/65/2/1/ Queen Mary Aberdeen University, Special Collections Centre).

forty-two-year-old John Orr, distinguished graduate in science and medicine, initially appointed in 1913, could finally embark on his role as director of what was destined to become a leading authority in human as well as animal nutrition.

Having subscribed to Napoleon's dictum that an army marches on its stomach Orr when an officer in the First World War sent his troops into the countryside to gather vegetables to make into nourishing soups; there is surely no doubt he was the man to run the Rowett.

Initially envisaged to service the farming community; to improve crop yields and stock rearing the Rowett quickly broadened its scope to embrace human nutrition – a role it fulfils to this day.

John Orr, later Boyd Orr – Popeye to his family – was a man of intelligence, humanity and strong resolve who did not recognise the word no. The son of an Ayrshire quarry owner, Orr had encountered poverty during his student days in Glasgow. The city's stunted and sickly population shocked and angered the young Orr who suspected poverty and malnutrition were linked and was determined to help tackle such injustice. His attitudes were not universally shared. Today it is taken for granted that what we eat affects our physical and mental wellbeing but when Orr embarked on his role at the Rowett the association was contested. A 1931 study by the University of Glasgow denied any such

The Rowett Institute staff, 1922, Orr seated centre (MSU1451/RRI/1/65/2/1/staff1922 Aberdeen University, Special Collections Centre).

relationship concluding the poor were less healthy because of hereditary factors; music to the ears of a government providing grossly insufficient welfare assistance.

The view from Aberdeen was altogether different. The Rowett produced evidence that lives could be improved by intervention – findings dismissed as 'fuss' by a government in denial over the extent of poverty in Britain. For Orr ringworm, bad teeth, rickets, stunted growth, poor eyesight and hearing prevalent among the working classes were not genetic but the consequences of poverty, insanitary overcrowded homes, unsafe working environments and starvation wages that could buy only the worst kinds of foods.

One of the Rowett's first research programmes targeted a group of sickly school children from in and around Aberdeen whose parents were too poor to afford to buy them milk. Milk prices were kept artificially high through an arrangement between dairy farmers and government and in order to prevent too much milk flooding the market 'surpluses' were poured down drains. Orr wanted it poured into children's bellies. The group was given free milk at school then re-examined and were seen to have indeed benefited from the milk's protein, calcium and vitamins so much so school milk was provided across Scotland from 1927 and later throughout the rest of Britain.

At the height of the Depression a 1935 study of families, mainly from Aberdeen and Dundee, compared diets across income groups to discover what, if any, differences there were between types of food consumed and wellbeing. Nearly 50 per cent of the sample could only afford a restricted diet despite spending a higher percentage of their incomes on food than the wealthiest. A lack of eggs, butter, milk, vegetables, fruit and meat resulted

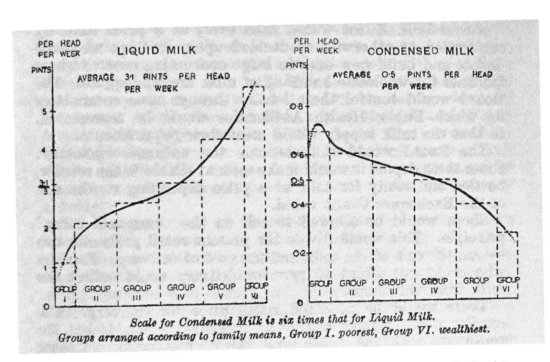

Scale for Condensed Milk is six times that for Liquid Milk.
Groups arranged according to family means, Group I. poorest, Group VI. wealthiest.

Graph showing intake of sugary milk compared with fresh milk by income, Sir John Boyd Orr, *Transactions of the Highlands and Agricultural Society of Scotland* (1938).

The Rowett during its early years.

in soft bones, small stature and deformities such as rickets and a greater susceptibility to infections, tuberculosis for example, at the time a major cause of death.

The results were embarrassing to the government who refused to publish them and when Boyd Orr threatened to do so privately he was informed he would be struck off the Medical Register if he went ahead. He refused to submit to blackmail and published. In 1936 *Food Health and Income: Report On a Survey of Adequacy of Diet in Relation to Income* grabbed public attention and became an international standard reference for students of social subjects but was condemned in some quarters for appearing to advocate a socialist redistribution of wealth:

> This new knowledge of nutrition, which shows that there can be an enormous improvement in the health and physique of the nation, coming at the same time as the greatly increased powers of producing food, has created an entirely new situation which demands economic statesmanship ... It is gratifying that the lead in this movement was taken by the British Empire.
>
> (FHI, 1936)

For the British Empire read Aberdeen and the Rowett. The 1935 study so impressed the Carnegie Trust it funded a more detailed survey of over 1,000 families across Scotland and

A laboratory at the Rowett, May 1930 (MSU1451/RRI/1/65LabSceneMay1930. Aberdeen University, Special Collections Centre).

England. It was scarcely complete at the outbreak of the Second World War and published as *Feeding the People in War-time* in 1940 by Boyd Orr and fellow Rowett scientist David Lubbock. Its findings contributed to the government's strategy for food rationing and Boyd Orr was taken onto Churchill's wartime Scientific Committee on Food Policy. The report recommended nutritional needs ought to be built into any food strategy for, as its findings revealed, one-third of the population already experienced rationing through lack of income. In order to lessen such inequality it advocated that basic nourishing food should be provided free or cheap to those most in need, including women and growing children.

> ... a rationing system which gave priority for milk and eggs to mothers and children and ensured that when a cargo of oranges came in, a millionaire could not get one until the poorest child in the slums had got sufficient for its needs.
>
> (FPW, 1940)

Boyd Orr's determination to highlight food's importance in our lives led to him setting up the Nutrition Society in 1941 to promote international scientific research into nutrition in human and animal health – a mirror of the Rowett's role but with a higher profile.

Milk was back on the agenda during the war. An article in the *Press and Journal* on 20 May 1944 headlined 'Commons Storm over Milk Scheme' claimed around 50 million

Sir John Boyd Orr: The Probable Effects on British Agriculture of the Recommendations of the United Nations Conference on Food and Agriculture Until about twenty-five years ago, it was generally assumed that if people had sufficient food to satisfy hunger, the needs of the body would be met. But discoveries in the field of nutrition showed that a number of diseases, the cause of which had long been a mystery, and also a good deal of ill-health prevalent, especially among the poor, were due to the lack of certain specific nutrients. Some foods, such as milk, dairy products, eggs, fruit, vegetables, meat, and fish are rich in these nutrients, and are called ' protective ' foods because they protect against disease. On the other hand, other foodstuffs, such as white bread, sugar, margarine, and jam, which satisfy hunger at low cost, are poor in these nutrients. Dietary surveys done in Britain in the 1930s showed that between a third and a half of the population did not eat sufficient of the protective foods for health. The main cause of the faulty diet was the fact that sufficient of the relatively expensive protective foods was beyond the purchasing power of poor families. Extract from: *Transactions of The Highland and Agricultural Society of Scotland, 1944*

Sir John Boyd Orr, *Transactions*, op.cit. (1944).

gallons of milk were lost annually through diseases in Britain's dairy herds but regardless of this malnutrition declined among Britain's poor during the war so that Boyd Orr could later claim, 'the women and children of the poorer classes were healthier at the end of the war than at the beginning of it.'

Fears that following the success of wartime rationing peace would bring a return to class inequalities in diet proved accurate. A survey begun before the war and published a decade after, in 1955, *Family Diet and Health in Pre-War Britain,* verified evidence that low incomes were linked to restricted varieties of food of inferior quality. Here was Want – one of the social evils taken into account when shaping the National Health Service. As good as the NHS became it was largely reactive in coping with health inequalities. A study in Aberdeen in 1970 showed the diets of the poor still to be inadequate with their children less likely to attain their growth and weight potential than children from better-off families. The findings exposed, too, that Boyd Orr's ambition for a national food policy linked to an agricultural programme designed to counter such wrongs was far from a priority for governments.

Boyd Orr was never reluctant to take the battle to counter malnutrition to the government of the day. On the occasion of the first United Nations conference to discuss food and agriculture with reference to US President Roosevelt's Four Freedoms of entitlement including Want, in 1943 at Hot Springs in America, Boyd Orr was refused official status by the British government fearful his 'unorthodox' views might commit the UK to participation in a world hunger relief programme for which they had no appetite. He stayed on despite the snub, in a private capacity.

When the USA later abandoned support for the UN's Food and Agricultural Organisation (FAO) following pressure from big business a disappointed Boyd Orr, on leaving the US, paused on the ship's gangway, took a handkerchief from his pocket, wiped

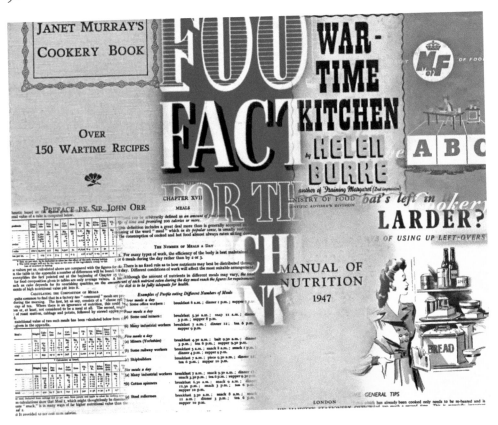

Wartime recipe books and nutrition guides (note plain Sir John Orr).

the dust of America off the soles of his shoes and dropped the handkerchief into the harbour.

Britain's post-war Labour government while progressive in some ways was as uninterested in cooperating on international food policies as previous administrations to the fury and frustration of Boyd Orr who in 1945 had become the UNFAO's first Director General. He could never understand the indifference of individuals and governments to starvation and malnutrition or those who put profit ahead of compassion.

Despite the obstacles placed in his path Boyd Orr never lost his determination to make a difference. Retiring from the Rowett at the end of the war he continued campaigning for food equality and world peace, tirelessly traversing the globe and rubbing governments up the wrong way. He met with world leaders from the Pope to Stalin in search of solutions to worldwide food poverty. In response to claims that greater investment in agriculture was an expense too far he suggested a 10 per cent reduction in military and space spending was all that was required to eliminate world famine. Boyd Orr argued hunger was man-made; people starved because it was economically more profitable to maintain an insufficiency of food to keep up prices. The man from the Rowett understood the cynical nature of food economics and when he condemned it he was accused of 'bringing politics into science,' as though they were separate.

PROBLEM OF OUR TIME: FROM LAND TO MOUTH

David Low cartoon illustrating Sir Boyd Orr's frustration at starvation in a world of food surpluses. First published in the *Evening Standard* on 26 August 1947 (courtesy of British Cartoon Archive, University of Kent, www.cartoons.ac.uk).

As a leading expert in nutrition science undaunted by officialdom Boyd Orr might have appeared an ideal first Director General of the UN's FAO. The fact is he found his plans stymied by member governments who dragged their feet and by the hugely bureaucratic organisation of the UN. In frustration he resigned to pursue his goals by other means such as a scheme to use up food surpluses and have worldwide food prices controlled centrally by the World Bank.

What he started with a tiny staff of four in a small building on the outskirts of Aberdeen grew into a remarkable centre of excellence in the pursuit of food production and nutrition. The Rowett's expansion into Strathcona House to accommodate the many overseas visitors who flocked to consult its distinguished Reid Library was testament to its international standing.

Boyd Orr's foresight in extending the Rowett's initial function from purely animal concerns to include human aspects of health sometimes led to surprising breakthroughs: greater understanding of toxaemia in pregnant women from work carried out on sheep; a reduction in piglet deaths from improving their environment and feeding could be equally applicable to human babies.

In recognition of his contribution to the Rowett's ground-breaking work, his personal crusade to eliminate world hunger and promote world peace the Scottish scientist Sir John Boyd Orr was awarded the Nobel Peace Prize in 1949. Perhaps unsurprisingly he

Sir Boyd Orr seated centre with Rowett staff in Nairobi in 1928 (MSU1451/RRI/1/65/ StaffInNairobiKenya. Aberdeen University, Special Collections Centre).

gave away the cash prize to peace organisations and those pursuing a united world government. Boyd Orr was made a Freeman of the City of Aberdeen that same year to add to the many honours bestowed upon him, including a knighthood in 1935 for the benefits his work brought Scottish children.

For a career he almost stumbled into Boyd Orr achieved great success as a proselytiser for equality, peace and agricultural policies developed on nutritional needs rather than economics: author of books and academic papers on agriculture and nutrition including *Nutrition Abstracts and Reviews*; popular lecturer in many countries; glad-hander of world leaders; broadcaster; founder of numerous bodies relating to diet and health including the International Food Council tackling post-war food shortages; founder of the World Academy of Art and Science which scrutinised scientific discoveries including nuclear weapons. The struggles he encountered as Director of the Rowett to convince governments to act on the institute's research findings were small beer compared with his battle to feed and unify the world.

The work of the Rowett was never parochial but always reached outward. Its scientists were inveterate world travellers dispensing advice and gathering information on agriculture and diet from the Middle East to the Americas and Africa to Australasia. In Kenya they investigated cattle grazing and the differing diets of the Kikuyu and Masai peoples. The Rowett helped establish food standard committees in forty countries through the auspices of the League of Nations and Boyd Orr was an adviser on agricultural affairs to both the Indian and Pakistani governments.

Rowett staff member with goat (MSU1451/RRI/1/65/8/6/goat. Aberdeen University, Special Collections Centre).

Boyd Orr's final public engagement was to open a large extension to the Rowett's laboratories in 1970. He died aged ninety at home in Brechin the following year but the institution that will always be associated with this giant of a man continues to leave its mark on the world.

Did You Know?

Lord Boyd Orr was not the only member of staff at the Rowett to receive a Nobel Prize. Among notable scientists employed there was J. J. R. MacLeod an Aberdeen graduate who joined the Rowett in 1928 as a consultant physiologist (he was also Regius Professor of Physiology at the University). MacLeod was a joint winner of the Nobel Prize for physiology or medicine in 1923 for his contribution to the discovery of insulin.

The Rowett's former head of the Department of Protein and Carbohydrate Chemistry, R. L. M. Synge, was also a joint winner of a Nobel Prize. In 1952 he shared the prize for chemistry, for the development of partition chromatography, particularly paper chromatography.

Acknowledgements

I am indebted to the following people for their assistance, advice and generosity: Susan Bell and David Oswald, Aberdeen City Libraries; Siobhán Convery, Andrew MacGregor, Neil Curtis and the staff at Special Collections, University of Aberdeen especially Michelle Gait for her endurance; Fiona Musk, NHS Grampian Archives; David Catto, Aberdeenshire Libraries. Special thanks go to Dr Hilary Hinton, Honorary Librarian, Aberdeen Medico-Chirurgical Society and staff at Med-Chi; Dr Maria Bergmann and Dr Andrew Wear for his invaluable guidance; to Jamie Dey for photographs; Sarah Richardson, British Cartoon Archive, University of Kent; finally my husband Dr Michael Dey for his invaluable knowledge of Aberdeen.